The Lost Bible of Herbal Healing

Ancient Wisdom for Modern Health.
Unlock the Power of Herbal Medicine with DIY Natural
Remedies, and Step-by-Step Recipes for Your Lifelong
Wellness

AMAZING EXTRA CONTENT INCLUDED:

- **40+ Hours of Uncutted Dr.Barbara Videos and Success Stories**

- **How to grow and prepare Medicinal Herbs at Home**

- **Step-by-Step Guide to Start Your Own Highly Profitable Herbal Business**

By Cedar Fireheart

Disclaimer:

The information contained in this book is for educational and informational purposes only and is not intended as health or medical advice. Always seek the advice of your physician or other qualified health provider with any questions you may have regarding a medical condition or treatment and before undertaking a new health care regimen. Do not disregard professional medical advice or delay in seeking it because of something you have read in this book.

The author and publisher are not responsible for any actions taken by readers as a result of reading this book. The content is provided on an "as is" basis, and the author and publisher make no representations or warranties of any kind, express or implied, regarding the accuracy, completeness, or suitability of the information contained herein.

Trademark Notice:

All product names, trademarks, and registered trademarks are property of their respective owners. All company, product, and service names used in this book are for identification purposes only. Use of these names, trademarks, and brands does not imply endorsement.

.

Table of Contents

Chapter 1: Introduction to Herbal Medicine

The Basics of Herbal Medicine: History and Evolution

Herbal medicine, often referred to as botanical medicine or phytotherapy, boasts a rich and diverse heritage that spans thousands of years. From the roots of ancient civilizations to the advancements of the modern era, herbs have consistently played a pivotal role in promoting healing and wellness.

Ancient Beginnings

The utilization of herbs for medicinal purposes can be traced back to prehistoric times, with archaeological findings indicating that humans have employed plants for healing for over 60,000 years. Ancient records from civilizations such as Egypt, China, and India extensively document the use of herbs. For instance, the Ebers Papyrus from Egypt, dating back to 1500 BCE, lists more than 700 plant-based remedies.

In ancient China, the foundational text "Shennong Ben Cao Jing" (The Divine Farmer's Materia Medica), attributed to the legendary Emperor Shennong around 2800 BCE, catalogs medicinal plants. Similarly, Ayurveda, India's traditional medicine system, has incorporated herbs for over 5,000 years with texts like the "Charaka Samhita" and "Sushruta Samhita" detailing the therapeutic uses of numerous plants.

The Greek and Roman Influence

The Greeks and Romans significantly enriched herbal medicine. Hippocrates, the "Father of Medicine," championed herbal remedies alongside diet and lifestyle adjustments. His axiom, "Let food be thy medicine and medicine be thy food," highlights the essence of natural healing.

Dioscorides, a Greek physician in the Roman army, compiled "De Materia Medica" in the 1st century CE, a seminal text describing over 600 plants and their uses. Galen, another influential Greek physician, built on Dioscorides' work, creating complex herbal formulas that shaped medical practices for centuries.

Medieval and Renaissance Developments

During the medieval period, monastic communities were vital in preserving and disseminating herbal knowledge. Monks in monastery gardens carefully documented and cultivated medicinal plants. The 12th-century German Benedictine abbess, Hildegard von Bingen, extensively discussed the healing properties of herbs in her works "Physica" and "Causae et Curae."

The Renaissance sparked a revival in botanical medicine, propelled by the printing press and new geographical discoveries. Herbalists like Nicholas Culpeper in England made plant knowledge widely accessible through works like "The Complete Herbal."

The Modern Era and Scientific Validation

The 19th and 20th centuries witnessed a transformative period where herbal medicine was subjected to scientific scrutiny. Pharmacognosy, the study of medicinal plants, evolved into a distinct discipline, with researchers isolating active plant compounds that led to the development of modern pharmaceuticals, such as aspirin from willow bark.

Today, the integration of traditional wisdom with scientific research underscores a balanced approach to healing, exemplified by the holistic use of whole plants. This perspective is increasingly embraced within integrative medicine, which merges traditional treatments with modern healthcare practices.

Herbal Medicine Today

Globally, herbal medicine remains a cornerstone of health care, with the World Health Organization (WHO) estimating that 80% of the world's population utilizes herbal remedies for some aspect of primary health care. In the West, there is a resurgence of interest in natural and holistic health methods, driven by concerns over synthetic medications' side effects and a preference for sustainable health solutions.

The importance of quality, purity, and informed usage of herbal remedies cannot be overstated, highlighting the necessity of consulting with knowledgeable health practitioners and sourcing herbs from reputable suppliers.

This chapter sets the stage for understanding herbal medicine's profound impact on health and wellness, blending ancient traditions with contemporary practices. The next chapter will explore how to prepare and use these herbal remedies effectively, focusing on safety and maximizing their therapeutic benefits.

Understanding Your Body's Needs

To effectively harness the power of herbal medicine, it's essential to understand your body's unique needs. This chapter will guide you through identifying your body's signals and understanding how to address them with herbal remedies.

Listening to Your Body

Our bodies are constantly communicating with us, signaling when something is out of balance. Symptoms such as fatigue, digestive issues, skin problems, and mood swings are not just random occurrences; they are messages that something needs attention.

1. **Identify Your Symptoms:**

    o   Keep a journal of your symptoms, noting the time of day, duration, and any associated activities or foods. This can help identify patterns and triggers.

2. **Assess Your Lifestyle:**

    o   Consider your diet, exercise routine, sleep patterns, and stress levels. These factors play a significant role in your overall health and can impact how your body responds to herbal remedies.

3. **Evaluate Your Environment:**

    o   Your surroundings, including your home, workplace, and community, can influence your health. Exposure to pollutants, allergens, and even negative social interactions can contribute to health issues.

Understanding Your Constitution

In herbal medicine, understanding your constitution or body type is crucial. Different people have different constitutions, which can influence how they respond to herbs. Barbara O'Neill teaches that knowing your constitution can help tailor remedies to your specific needs.

1. **Ayurvedic Constitutions:**

    o   Ayurveda, the traditional medicine system of India, classifies individuals into three main types or doshas: Vata, Pitta, and Kapha. Each dosha has its characteristics and tendencies, and imbalances can lead to specific health issues.

    o   **Vata**: Typically thin and energetic, but prone to anxiety and digestive issues.

    o   **Pitta**: Medium build with a strong appetite, but may experience inflammation and irritability.

    o   **Kapha**: Heavier build, calm demeanor, but may struggle with sluggishness and congestion.

2. **Traditional Chinese Medicine (TCM) Constitutions:**

    o   TCM also categorizes people into different types based on elements such as wood, fire, earth, metal, and water. Each element correlates with specific organs and health tendencies.

    o   **Wood**: Creative and ambitious but prone to stress and liver issues.

    o   **Fire**: Passionate and energetic but may face heart-related problems.

- o **Earth**: Nurturing and stable but can experience digestive issues.

- o **Metal**: Organized and disciplined but might suffer from respiratory problems.

- o **Water**: Reflective and adaptable but could have kidney or urinary issues.

Personalized Herbal Strategies

With a deeper understanding of your symptoms and constitution, you can adopt a more tailored approach to using herbal remedies. This section promotes the development of individualized herbal strategies that cater directly to your specific needs.

1. **Customizing Herbal Blends:**

   - o Select herbs that align with your constitution and symptoms. For instance, Vata types may benefit from warming and grounding herbs like ginger and ashwagandha, while Pitta types might need cooling herbs like peppermint and aloe vera.

2. **Integrating Dietary Adjustments:**

   - o Complement herbal remedies with dietary changes that support your constitution. Vata individuals should focus on warm, nourishing foods, while Pitta types might thrive on cooling, hydrating meals. Kapha types should incorporate light, spicy foods to boost metabolism.

3. **Adapting Lifestyle Practices:**

   - o Incorporate daily routines and activities that harmonize your body type. Vata individuals should ensure regular rest and structured schedules, Pitta personalities might find peace in mindfulness and meditation, and Kapha types should engage in regular physical activity and invigorating pursuits.

Case Studies and Real-Life Examples

To demonstrate the real-world efficacy of these principles, we explore several case studies that showcase how a deep understanding of individual body needs facilitates effective herbal treatments.

1. **Case Study 1: Digestive Issues**

   - o Jane, who aligns with the Pitta constitution, had been suffering from chronic acid reflux. By recognizing her body type and its triggers, she began using cooling herbs like licorice root and made dietary adjustments to avoid spicy foods, which are known irritants for Pitta types. These changes led to a significant improvement in her symptoms within a few weeks.

2. **Case Study 2: Anxiety and Insomnia**

- Tom, identified as a Vata type, struggled with severe anxiety and insomnia. With insights into his constitution, Tom introduced calming herbs such as valerian root into his routine and implemented a bedtime ritual that included warm baths and gentle yoga. These modifications significantly enhanced his sleep quality and reduced his anxiety levels.

3. **Case Study 3: Respiratory Problems**

   - Sarah, characterized by the Metal constitution in Traditional Chinese Medicine, frequently battled respiratory infections. Upon acknowledging her specific body type, she incorporated herbs like mullein, which support respiratory health, and adjusted her diet to decrease mucus production. These steps gradually fortified her respiratory system.

Recognizing and responding to your body's specific needs is fundamental to effective herbal medicine. By attuning to your body's messages, identifying your constitutional type, and tailoring your healthcare practices, you can attain improved health outcomes. The teachings stress the importance of this personalized approach, empowering you to manage your health naturally and proactively.

As we continue, subsequent chapters will delve into the details of specific herbs and their uses, providing guidance on how to prepare and utilize them effectively. This exploration into herbal medicine is designed not merely to address symptoms but to foster holistic well-being for enduring health.

Principles of Herbal Wellness

Herbal wellness, is grounded in the understanding that nature provides a vast array of plants capable of supporting and enhancing our health. The principles of herbal wellness involve harnessing the therapeutic properties of herbs to promote balance and healing within the body. This chapter will explore these principles in detail, providing a comprehensive understanding of how to integrate herbal remedies into your daily life effectively.

Holistic Approach to Health

One of the core principles of herbal wellness is the holistic approach to health. Barbara O'Neill often emphasizes that true health is not merely the absence of disease but a state of complete physical, mental, and emotional well-being. Herbal medicine aims to treat the whole person, considering all aspects of their lifestyle and environment.

1. **Treating the Root Cause:**

   - Herbal wellness focuses on addressing the underlying causes of health issues rather than merely alleviating symptoms. For example, instead of just treating a headache with a painkiller, herbalists seek to understand and address the root cause, whether it's stress, dehydration, or dietary deficiencies.

2. **Balance and Harmony:**

o   Herbs are used to restore balance and harmony within the body. This principle is rooted in the belief that the body has an innate ability to heal itself when given the right support. Herbs can help rebalance bodily systems, such as the digestive, nervous, and immune systems.

Individualized Care

Each person is unique, with different constitutions, lifestyles, and health needs. Personalized herbal remedies are tailored to meet these specific needs.

1. **Constitutional Analysis:**

   o   Understanding an individual's constitution is crucial for effective herbal treatment. This involves assessing factors such as body type, temperament, and specific health tendencies. For instance, someone with a cold, damp constitution might benefit from warming and drying herbs like ginger and cinnamon.

2. **Personalized Remedies:**

   o   Herbal wellness involves creating personalized remedies that cater to an individual's unique health profile. This might include custom herbal blends, dietary recommendations, and lifestyle modifications.

Synergy and Whole Plant Use

Another fundamental principle is the use of whole plants and the synergy of their components. Using the whole plant, rather than isolated extracts, ensures a balanced and effective remedy.

1. **Whole Plant Medicine:**

   o   Whole plant medicine takes advantage of the synergistic effects of all the plant's constituents. This means that the various compounds in the plant work together to enhance the overall therapeutic effect and reduce the risk of side effects.

2. **Herbal Combinations:**

   o   Combining different herbs can create a synergistic effect, where the combined action of the herbs is greater than the sum of their individual effects. For example, combining valerian root and passionflower can provide a more comprehensive treatment for insomnia than either herb alone.

Prevention and Maintenance

Herbal wellness extends beyond merely addressing current health issues; it also encompasses preventive care and ongoing maintenance. It is often recommended to incorporate herbal remedies into a daily wellness routine to both sustain good health and avert potential ailments. This approach to holistic health not only treats but actively works to prevent health issues before they begin.

1. **Daily Herbal Support:**

    o   Incorporating herbs into daily routines can support overall health and prevent the onset of disease. This might include drinking herbal teas, using herbal supplements, or incorporating medicinal herbs into meals.

2. **Seasonal Adjustments:**

    o   Adjusting herbal use according to the seasons can help maintain balance and prevent illness. For instance, using warming herbs like cinnamon and ginger in the winter and cooling herbs like mint and chamomile in the summer.

Integration with Modern Medicine

Integrating herbal wellness with modern medicine is crucial for achieving optimal health outcomes. While herbs offer significant health benefits, their effectiveness is maximized when used alongside conventional medical care.

1. **Complementary Approach:**

    o   Herbal wellness can enhance modern medical treatments, providing additional support and improving overall health. For instance, herbs like milk thistle can bolster liver health during conventional treatments, creating a more holistic approach to healing.

2. **Informed Choices:**

    o   Understanding the potential interactions between herbs and pharmaceuticals is essential. Consulting with healthcare professionals ensures the safe and effective use of herbal remedies in conjunction with conventional treatments, helping to avoid adverse interactions and maximize therapeutic benefits.

By combining the strengths of both herbal and modern medicine, individuals can achieve a balanced and comprehensive approach to health and wellness.

Practical Application of Herbal Principles

To bring these principles into practice, it's essential to start with small, manageable steps and gradually integrate more herbs into your daily life. Here are some practical applications:

1. **Start with Teas and Infusions:**

o   Herbal teas and infusions are a simple and effective way to begin incorporating herbs into your routine. Chamomile tea for relaxation, peppermint tea for digestion, and nettle tea for overall health are excellent starting points.

2. **Create a Herbal Medicine Cabinet:**

   o   Building a basic herbal medicine cabinet with essential herbs like echinacea for immune support, ginger for digestive health, and lavender for stress relief can provide quick access to natural remedies.

3. **Daily Rituals:**

   o   Incorporate herbal rituals into your daily life, such as a morning tea ritual, using herbal oils for skin care, or adding fresh herbs to meals. These small changes can significantly impact your overall well-being.

Understanding your body's needs and applying the principles of herbal wellness can lead to a more balanced and healthy life. By treating the whole person, focusing on prevention, and integrating herbs into daily routines, you can harness the full potential of herbal medicine.

Chapter 2: Comprehensive Herbal Remedies Guide

In this chapter, we delve deep into the heart of natural healing, exploring the myriad of herbs that form the backbone of traditional and contemporary herbal medicine. This guide offers a comprehensive perspective on using herbal remedies effectively. This approach blends ancient wisdom with modern practices to present a balanced and thorough understanding of herbal wellness.

Understanding Herbal Synergy

Herbs have played a vital role in healing, nourishing, and balancing the human body for centuries. Their effectiveness is rooted not only in their unique individual properties but also in their remarkable ability to work synergistically with other herbs and treatments. This synergistic effect amplifies the benefits of each herb, creating a more potent and balanced approach to health and wellness.

This holistic perspective is essential for understanding how to best utilize herbs for optimal health. Rather than focusing on isolated symptoms, this approach considers the whole person—mind, body, and spirit—and how various elements of health are interconnected. By recognizing that herbs can complement each other and conventional treatments, we can harness their full potential to support and enhance our well-being.

A key aspect of this holistic approach is the belief that our bodies function best when supported in a comprehensive and cohesive manner. This means integrating herbal remedies into a broader lifestyle that includes proper nutrition, exercise, stress management, and other healthy habits. By doing so, we create an environment in which our bodies can heal and thrive naturally.

For instance, combining herbs that support different bodily systems can lead to more effective outcomes. A blend of adaptogenic herbs, which help the body manage stress, with anti-inflammatory herbs, which reduce inflammation, can provide a well-rounded approach to improving overall health. Additionally, using herbs in conjunction with modern medical treatments can enhance their efficacy and reduce side effects, leading to a more balanced and integrated approach to health care.

In essence, the holistic approach to herbal medicine underscores the importance of treating the whole person rather than just addressing individual symptoms. By understanding the synergistic potential of herbs and incorporating them into a comprehensive health regimen, we can achieve a more profound and lasting impact on our overall well-being. This philosophy aligns with the belief that our bodies are best supported when we take a complete and cohesive approach to health.

Building Your Herbal Toolkit

An essential part of using herbal remedies is knowing which herbs are suited for specific conditions. This section of the guide provides detailed descriptions of key herbs, including their historical uses, active constituents, and how they interact with the body. We cover a wide spectrum, from well-known herbs like ginger and turmeric, which are celebrated for their anti-inflammatory properties, to lesser-known ones like ashwagandha, which is revered in Ayurvedic medicine for its stress-reducing effects.

Safe and Effective Use of Herbs

Using herbs safely and effectively requires careful consideration and respect for their natural potency. While herbs offer numerous health benefits, it is important to approach their use with knowledge and caution to maximize their therapeutic effects and minimize potential risks. Here are some key guidelines for the safe and effective use of herbs:

1. Educate Yourself

Understanding the properties, benefits, and potential side effects of herbs is crucial before incorporating them into your health routine. Use reliable sources such as herbal medicine books, scientific research articles, and advice from qualified herbalists or healthcare professionals to gather accurate information.

2. Consult with Healthcare Professionals

Before starting any new herbal treatment, especially if you have pre-existing health conditions, are pregnant or nursing, or are taking other medications, consult with a healthcare professional or a qualified herbalist. Professional guidance ensures that the herbs you use are appropriate for your specific health needs and do not interact negatively with other treatments.

3. Start with Low Doses

When introducing a new herb into your routine, begin with a low dose to observe how your body responds. Gradually increase the dosage as needed, following recommended guidelines. This cautious approach helps minimize the risk of adverse reactions and allows you to monitor the herb's effects on your body.

4. Be Aware of Potential Interactions

Herbs can interact with other herbs, medications, and certain foods. It is essential to be aware of these potential interactions to avoid unwanted side effects. For instance, some herbs can enhance the effects of blood thinners, while others may interfere with the absorption of certain medications. Always check for potential interactions and seek professional advice if you are unsure.

5. Use High-Quality Herbs

The quality of the herbs you use is crucial for their effectiveness and safety. Choose herbs from reputable sources that provide information about their sourcing, cultivation, and processing methods. Organic and wild-crafted herbs are often preferred for their purity and potency.

6. Follow Proper Preparation Methods

Different herbs require different preparation methods to unlock their full therapeutic potential. Whether you are making teas, tinctures, infusions, or decoctions, follow the recommended preparation methods for each herb. Proper preparation ensures that you extract the beneficial compounds effectively and safely.

7. Monitor Your Body's Response

Pay close attention to how your body responds to herbal treatments. Keeping a journal to track any changes in symptoms, side effects, or overall health can be helpful. This practice allows you and your healthcare professional to adjust dosages or switch herbs if necessary.

8. Respect the Power of Herbs

Herbs are potent natural remedies, and it is essential to respect their power. Avoid exceeding recommended dosages and duration of use. Long-term or excessive use of certain herbs can lead to adverse effects or reduce their efficacy.

9. Stay Informed About Safety Guidelines

Herbal medicine is an evolving field, with ongoing research providing new insights into the safety and efficacy of different herbs. Stay informed about the latest guidelines and recommendations from reputable sources to ensure that you are using herbs safely and effectively.

10. Use Herbs as Part of a Holistic Approach

Incorporate herbal remedies as part of a holistic approach to health that includes a balanced diet, regular exercise, adequate rest, and stress management. Herbs can enhance your overall well-being when used in conjunction with other healthy lifestyle practices.

By following these guidelines, you can safely and effectively harness the healing power of herbs, supporting your journey toward optimal health and well-being. Remember, herbal medicine is a powerful tool that, when used responsibly, can provide profound benefits for your health.

Detailed Profiles of 100+ Key Herbs: Uses and Benefits

Acai Berry (Euterpe oleracea)

- **Overview:** Native to the rainforests of South America, acai berries are renowned for their high antioxidant content, which surpasses that of other berries. These dark purple fruits are used both nutritionally and medicinally.

- **Active Compounds:** Rich in anthocyanins, polyphenols, and vitamins A, C, and E.

- **Different Uses Against Diseases:** Acai berries are used to promote heart health, aid in weight loss, enhance skin health, and improve cellular health. They have anti-aging effects and are believed to help with cholesterol management.

- **Preparation Methods, Dosage, Safety, and Precautions:** Acai is typically consumed as a juice or pulp in smoothies and bowls. Supplements are available as pills or powders. It's generally safe, but moderation is advised due to its potent effects. Always check for potential interactions with other medications, especially anticoagulants.

Alfalfa (Medicago sativa)

- **Overview:** Alfalfa is a perennial flowering plant often used in herbal medicine. It is rich in vitamins and minerals and used to support overall health.

- **Active Compounds:** Contains vitamins A, C, E, and K4; minerals like potassium, phosphorus, and iron; and saponins.

- **Different Uses Against Diseases:** Traditionally used to detoxify the body, support urinary and kidney health, lower cholesterol, and promote better hormonal balance.

- **Preparation Methods, Dosage, Safety, and Precautions:** Leaves can be eaten in salads or dried and taken as tea. Seeds and sprouted seeds are edible but should be consumed in moderation due to potential toxicity. Pregnant women should avoid using alfalfa supplements due to their potential estrogenic effects.

Aloe Vera (Aloe barbadensis)

- **Overview:** A succulent plant species from the genus Aloe. It grows abundantly in tropical climates and has been used for centuries for its health, beauty, medicinal, and skincare properties.

- **Active Compounds:** Contains vitamins A, C, and E; enzymes; minerals like zinc and selenium; amino acids; and salicylic acids.

- **Different Uses Against Diseases:** Aloe vera is best known for its topical application to soothe burns, heal wounds, and moisturize skin. Internally, it can help with digestion and relieve constipation.

- **Preparation Methods, Dosage, Safety, and Precautions:** Aloe vera gel can be applied directly to the skin or consumed in juice form. It should not be ingested in high doses due to potential laxative effects and kidney issues.

Amaranth (Amaranthus spp.)

- **Overview:** An ancient grain that was a staple food of the Aztecs and is known for its nutty flavor and high nutritional value.

- **Active Compounds:** Rich in fiber, protein, micronutrients like manganese, magnesium, iron, and selenium.

- **Different Uses Against Diseases:** Amaranth is praised for its cardiovascular benefits, ability to reduce inflammation, and support for digestive health. It's also beneficial for lowering cholesterol levels.

- **Preparation Methods, Dosage, Safety, and Precautions:** Can be consumed as a grain similar to quinoa, added to salads, or used to make porridge. It's gluten-free, making it a great alternative for those with gluten sensitivities.

Anise (Pimpinella anisum)

- **Overview:** Anise is a flowering plant native to the eastern Mediterranean and Southwest Asia. Its seeds are used for flavoring and its medicinal properties.

- **Active Compounds:** Anethole, which is responsible for its distinct licorice-like flavor and has been shown to have antifungal and antibacterial properties.

- **Different Uses Against Diseases:** It is commonly used to treat digestive issues such as bloating, gas, indigestion, and irritable bowel syndrome. It is also used to alleviate symptoms of menopause and menstrual discomfort.

- **Preparation Methods, Dosage, Safety, and Precautions:** Typically consumed as a tea or used as a spice in cooking. It should be used in moderation as excessive consumption can lead to allergic reactions and interactions with other medications.

Apple Cider Vinegar (Acetic acid from apples)

- **Overview**: Made from fermented apple juice, apple cider vinegar is used for its health benefits and as a popular home remedy.

- **Active Compounds**: Contains acetic acid, which has antimicrobial properties, as well as trace amounts of other acids, vitamins, and minerals.

- **Different Uses Against Diseases**: Promotes weight loss, improved digestion, and blood sugar control. It is also used for its detoxifying properties and can help with skin conditions like acne.

- **Preparation Methods, Dosage, Safety, and Precautions**: Often diluted with water before consumption to protect tooth enamel and the esophagus. It should be used with caution if you have kidney problems or are taking diuretics.

Artemisia (Artemisia annua)

- **Overview**: Also known as sweet wormwood, Artemisia is used in traditional Chinese medicine and is known for its role in the treatment of malaria.

- **Active Compounds**: Contains artemisinin, which is effective against malaria-causing parasites.

- **Different Uses Against Diseases**: Apart from its antimalarial properties, it is used to combat fever, inflammation, and bacterial infections.

- **Preparation Methods, Dosage, Safety, and Precautions**: Available in capsules, tablets, and tea forms. The dosage should be controlled especially in the treatment of malaria, under medical supervision to prevent resistance. Not recommended for pregnant women due to potential toxicity.

Ashitaba (Angelica keiskei)

- **Overview**: Native to Japan, Ashitaba is celebrated for its longevity properties and is often used in traditional Asian medicine. It is rich in a variety of phytonutrients and is known for its rapid regrowth capabilities.

protect plants from germs, bugs, fungi aka phytochemicals

- **Active Compounds**: Contains chalconoids, a type of flavonoid that exhibits strong antioxidant properties.

- **Different Uses Against Diseases**: Ashitaba is used for revitalizing energy and cleansing blood. It's also reputed to aid in digestion, improve joint health, and support endocrine health.

- **Preparation Methods, Dosage, Safety, and Precautions:** Often consumed as tea or added to food as a leafy vegetable. Regular consumption in moderate amounts is generally safe, but due to its potent effects, it should be used cautiously in pregnant women and those on anticoagulant therapy.

Asparagus Root (Asparagus racemosus)

- **Overview:** Known commonly as Shatavari, asparagus root is revered in Ayurvedic medicine as an adaptogenic herb.

- **Active Compounds:** Contains saponins, asparagine, and mucilage, which contribute to its medicinal qualities.

- **Different Uses Against Diseases:** Widely used to support reproductive health in women, enhance fertility, and regulate hormones. It also acts as a diuretic and is used to treat ulcers and digestive problems.

- **Preparation Methods, Dosage, Safety, and Precautions:** Available in powdered form or as a dietary supplement. Dosage should align with individual health needs and medical advice. Generally safe, but consultation with a healthcare provider is recommended for pregnant women or those with estrogen-sensitive conditions.

Arnica (Arnica montana)

- **Overview:** Arnica is a perennial, herbaceous plant in the sunflower family, known for its yellow, daisy-like flowers and used primarily for its anti-inflammatory properties.

- **Active Compounds:** Contains helenalin, a potent anti-inflammatory compound, along with thymol and flavonoids.

- **Different Uses Against Diseases:** Primarily used topically for bruises, sprains, and muscle aches. It is also applied to reduce arthritic pain and swelling due to fractures.

- **Preparation Methods, Dosage, Safety, and Precautions:** Commonly used in creams and ointments. Should not be applied to broken skin or ingested unless in homeopathic dosages due to its toxicity when consumed in larger amounts.

Astragalus (Astragalus membranaceus)

- **Overview:** A staple in Traditional Chinese Medicine, astragalus is known for its immune-boosting and anti-aging properties.

- **Active Compounds:** Rich in polysaccharides and saponins that enhance the immune system and support heart health. *polycarbohydrates* *glycosides et triterpenes and steroids*

- **Different Uses Against Diseases:** Commonly used to boost the immune system, support cardiovascular health, and as a general tonic to increase overall vitality.

- **Preparation Methods, Dosage, Safety, and Precautions:** Often taken as an extract, in teas, or as capsules. Long-term use is considered safe under guidance, but it should be avoided during acute infections and by those on immune-suppressing drugs.

Bacopa (Bacopa monnieri)

- **Overview:** Also known as Brahmi, this aquatic plant is famed in Ayurvedic medicine for its cognitive-enhancing properties.

- **Active Compounds:** Contains bacosides, which are credited with improving neural communication and antioxidant activity in the brain.

- **Different Uses Against Diseases:** Bacopa is primarily used to enhance memory, reduce anxiety, and improve concentration levels.

- **Preparation Methods, Dosage, Safety, and Precautions:** Can be taken as a tea, tablet, or tincture. Standard dosages vary but typically range from 300-450 mg of extract per day. Safe for most users, but it may cause gastrointestinal discomfort in some and should be used under medical advice for those on thyroid medication.

Barberry (Berberis vulgaris)

- **Overview:** Known for its bright yellow roots and bark, barberry is used for its antibacterial and anti-inflammatory properties.

- **Active Compounds:** Contains berberine, an alkaloid effective in fighting infections and improving gastrointestinal health.

- **Different Uses Against Diseases:** Used to treat digestive issues, urinary tract infections, and can help manage diabetes by lowering blood sugar levels.

- **Preparation Methods, Dosage, Safety, and Precautions:** Available in capsules, tinctures, and as a dried herb. Should be used cautiously as high doses can cause stomach upset, cramping, and an increased risk of jaundice in newborns if taken during pregnancy.

Basil (Ocimum basilicum)

- **Overview:** This common kitchen herb is not only culinary but also offers substantial medicinal benefits.

- **Active Compounds:** Rich in essential oils like eugenol which provides anti-inflammatory and antibacterial properties.

- **Different Uses Against Diseases:** Effective in treating digestive disorders, inflammation, and can provide relief from anxiety and depression.

- **Preparation Methods, Dosage, Safety, and Precautions:** Can be consumed fresh in meals, as a tea, or extracted into oil. Generally safe when used in food amounts; essential oil use should be diluted and used externally.

Bay Leaf (Laurus nobilis)

- **Overview:** More than just a flavoring agent, bay leaf has properties that benefit digestion and respiratory conditions.

- **Active Compounds:** Contains compounds like cineole and parthenolide, which have anti-inflammatory and antioxidant effects.

- **Different Uses Against Diseases:** Helps improve digestion, relieve respiratory conditions, and reduce inflammation.

- **Preparation Methods, Dosage, Safety, and Precautions:** Typically used in cooking but can be brewed as a tea. Whole leaves should be removed from food before consumption to prevent choking hazards.

Bilberry (Vaccinium myrtillus)

- **Overview:** A relative of the blueberry, bilberry fruits are known for their role in improving vision and vascular health.

- **Active Compounds:** Rich in anthocyanins, potent antioxidants that help strengthen blood vessels and improve eye health.

- **Different Uses Against Diseases:** Commonly used to enhance night vision, treat diabetic retinopathy, and improve circulation.

- **Preparation Methods, Dosage, Safety, and Precautions:** Often consumed as fruit, extract, or in capsules. While generally safe, it's advisable to consult a healthcare provider before starting, particularly for those on blood-thinning medications.

Bitter Melon (Momordica charantia)

- **Overview:** Known for its distinctive bitter flavor, this fruit is revered in traditional medicine for its anti-diabetic properties.

- **Active Compounds:** Contains charantin, vicine, and polypeptide-p, all known to lower blood sugar levels.

- **Different Uses Against Diseases:** Primarily used for managing diabetes and improving glucose tolerance.

- **Preparation Methods, Dosage, Safety, and Precautions:** Can be cooked and eaten as part of meals or taken as a supplement. Due to its potent effect on blood glucose levels, monitoring under a healthcare provider is recommended, especially for diabetics.

Bladderwrack (Fucus vesiculosus)

- **Overview:** A type of seaweed, bladderwrack is a source of iodine and has been used to treat thyroid issues.

- **Active Compounds:** Rich in iodine, fucoidan, and algin.

- **Different Uses Against Diseases:** Used to manage thyroid function, especially in cases of hypothyroidism, and to promote weight loss.

- **Preparation Methods, Dosage, Safety, and Precautions:** Available as a dried herb or supplement. Due to its high iodine content, it must be used under professional supervision to avoid potential thyroid imbalance.

Bloodroot (Sanguinaria canadensis)

- **Overview:** Native to North America, bloodroot is traditionally used for its antimicrobial and anti-inflammatory properties.

- **Active Compounds:** Contains sanguinarine, an alkaloid that can inhibit bacterial growth and has antiseptic properties.

- **Different Uses Against Diseases:** Applied topically for skin conditions like warts and fungal infections; also studied for its potential in treating respiratory conditions.

- **Preparation Methods, Dosage, Safety, and Precautions:** Primarily used in topical applications. Bloodroot should be used with extreme caution as it is highly potent and can be toxic if ingested.

Boldo (Peumus boldus)

- **Overview:** An important herb in Chilean medicine, boldo is used for its benefits to the liver and gallbladder.

- **Active Compounds:** Contains boldine, which has antioxidant and liver-protective effects.

- **Different Uses Against Diseases:** Traditionally used to treat digestive disorders and promote liver health.

- **Preparation Methods, Dosage, Safety, and Precautions:** Often consumed as a tea. It should be used cautiously, as excessive consumption can lead to liver damage and other serious health issues.

Borage (Borago officinalis)

- **Overview:** Known for its striking blue flowers, borage is valued for its anti-inflammatory and mood-lifting properties.

- **Active Compounds:** Rich in gamma-linolenic acid (GLA), a fatty acid that helps reduce inflammation.

- **Different Uses Against Diseases:** Used to relieve inflammation, improve skin health, and reduce symptoms of arthritis and other inflammatory conditions.

- **Preparation Methods, Dosage, Safety, and Precautions:** Borage oil is commonly taken in capsule form. Due to potential liver toxicity, the use of borage should be monitored, especially concerning the presence of pyrrolizidine alkaloids.

Calendula (Calendula officinalis)

- **Overview:** Renowned for its healing abilities, especially in skin care and wound healing.

- **Active Compounds:** Rich in flavonoids and carotenoids, which contribute to its anti-inflammatory and healing properties.

- **Different Uses Against Diseases:** Used topically for cuts, burns, bruises, and skin infections. Also, helps in treating sore throats when used as a gargle.

- **Preparation Methods, Dosage, Safety, and Precautions:** Can be used as creams, ointments, or a tea. It is very gentle and generally safe for most people, including in cosmetic applications.

Cardamom (Elettaria cardamomum)

- **Overview:** Often referred to as the "queen of spices," cardamom is not only culinary but also has medicinal uses, particularly for digestive health.

- **Active Compounds:** Contains cineole, which can enhance digestive enzyme secretion and reduce gas.

- **Different Uses Against Diseases:** Effective in combating nausea, bloating, acid reflux, and other digestive discomforts.

- **Preparation Methods, Dosage, Safety, and Precautions:** Commonly used as a spice in cooking or as a tea. Cardamom is generally safe, but excessive use can lead to gallstone issues due to its high cineole content.

Catnip (Nepeta cataria)

- **Overview:** Best known for its effects on cats, catnip also offers significant benefits for humans, primarily for relaxation and sleep.

- **Active Compounds:** Contains nepetalactone, which is responsible for its calming effects.

- **Different Uses Against Diseases:** Used to alleviate stress, anxiety, and insomnia. Also helpful in treating fever and cold symptoms.

- **Preparation Methods, Dosage, Safety, and Precautions:** Often consumed as a tea. Safe for most individuals, but pregnant women should avoid it due to potential uterine contractions.

Cat's Claw (Uncaria tomentosa)

- **Overview:** Indigenous to the Amazon rainforest, this vine is used primarily for its immune-boosting and anti-inflammatory properties.

- **Active Compounds:** Contains oxindole alkaloids that enhance immune function and reduce inflammation.

- **Different Uses Against Diseases:** Often used to boost immune response, fight viral infections, and reduce arthritis symptoms.

- **Preparation Methods, Dosage, Safety, and Precautions:** Available as capsules, tea, or tincture. Not recommended for pregnant or lactating women, and those with autoimmune diseases should use it cautiously.

apsicum annuum)

enowned for its heat and medicinal benefits, cayenne pepper is a powerful circulatory

ompounds: Capsaicin is the key compound, known for its pain-relieving properties.

erent Uses Against Diseases: Used topically as a pain reliever for arthritis and muscle aches, and internally to boost circulation and aid digestion.

- **Preparation Methods, Dosage, Safety, and Precautions:** Can be used in cooking or as a supplement. It should be used with caution due to its intense heat, which can irritate the skin and mucous membranes.

Celery Seed (Apium graveolens)

- **Overview:** Celery seeds are well-regarded in traditional medicine for their anti-inflammatory and diuretic properties.

- **Active Compounds:** Rich in volatile oils, flavonoids, and linoleic acid.

- **Different Uses Against Diseases:** Commonly used for reducing hypertension, alleviating arthritis symptoms, and promoting urinary tract health.

- **Preparation Methods, Dosage, Safety, and Precautions:** Can be taken as a spice in foods, in capsule form, or as a tea. It should be used cautiously by those with kidney disorders due to its diuretic effect.

Chaga (Inonotus obliquus)

- **Overview:** A fungus that grows on birch trees, chaga is prized for its antioxidant properties and immune support.

- **Active Compounds:** Contains a high content of superoxide dismutase (SOD), beta-glucans, and melanin.

- **Different Uses Against Diseases:** Known for boosting the immune system, fighting inflammation, and potentially reducing cancer risk.

- **Preparation Methods, Dosage, Safety, and Precautions:** Typically consumed as a tea. It's important to source chaga sustainably due to its slow growth rate. Generally safe, but long-term effects are not well studied.

Chamomile (Matricaria recutita)

- **Overview:** A well-loved herb known for its calming and anti-inflammatory effects, commonly used to aid sleep and digestion.

- **Active Compounds:** Contains bisabolol, flavonoids, and apigenin, which contribute to its soothing properties.

- **Different Uses Against Diseases:** Effective in treating insomnia, digestive upset, skin irritations, and anxiety.

- **Preparation Methods, Dosage, Safety, and Precautions:** Chamomile can be consumed as tea or used topically in creams and ointments. Generally safe, although allergic reactions can occur in individuals sensitive to the Asteraceae family.

Chlorella (Chlorella vulgaris)

- **Overview:** A freshwater algae, chlorella is a nutritional powerhouse that detoxifies and enhances overall health.

- **Active Compounds:** High in chlorophyll, protein, iron, vitamins, and minerals.

- **Different Uses Against Diseases:** Used to detoxify heavy metals from the body, boost immune function, and improve cholesterol levels.

- **Preparation Methods, Dosage, Safety, and Precautions:** Typically consumed as a powder or in tablet form. It's important to start with small doses due to its potent detoxifying effects.

Cinnamon (Cinnamomum verum)

- **Overview:** More than just a popular spice, cinnamon is used for its anti-inflammatory, antimicrobial, and antioxidant properties.

- **Active Compounds:** Contains cinnamaldehyde, which contributes to its health benefits.

- **Different Uses Against Diseases:** Known to help regulate blood sugar levels, reduce cholesterol, and combat neurodegenerative diseases.

- **Preparation Methods, Dosage, Safety, and Precautions:** Can be used in cooking or as a supplement. Ceylon cinnamon is preferred over Cassia due to lower coumarin content, which can be harmful in large doses.

Clove (Syzygium aromaticum)

- **Overview:** Cloves are used for their powerful antiseptic and pain-relieving properties, especially in dental care.

- **Active Compounds:** High in eugenol, which has pain-relieving and antibacterial effects.

- **Different Uses Against Diseases:** Effective in dental care for easing toothache and gum pain, and as a general antimicrobial.

- **Preparation Methods, Dosage, Safety, and Precautions:** Can be applied topically as an oil or consumed in small quantities in foods. Clove oil must be diluted and used carefully as it can irritate skin and mucous membranes.

Codonopsis (Codonopsis pilosula)

- **Overview:** Often used as a cheaper alternative to ginseng, Codonopsis boosts energy and supports immune health.

- **Active Compounds:** Contains saponins, which are similar to those found in ginseng, promoting health benefits.

- **Different Uses Against Diseases:** Used to enhance energy, improve appetite, and boost the immune system.

- **Preparation Methods, Dosage, Safety, and Precautions:** Commonly used in soups and teas. Generally considered safe, but should be used cautiously by those with autoimmune diseases.

Coltsfoot (Tussilago farfara)

- **Overview:** Traditionally used in Europe for respiratory conditions, coltsfoot helps to relieve cough and soothe sore throats.

- **Active Compounds:** Contains mucilage, tannins, and flavonoids that help reduce inflammation and support mucous membranes.

- **Different Uses Against Diseases:** Used to treat coughs, asthma, and bronchial issues.

- **Preparation Methods, Dosage, Safety, and Precautions:** Typically consumed as a tea. Due to concerns about pyrrolizidine alkaloids, which can be toxic to the liver, it should be used with caution and not recommended for long-term use.

Comfrey (Symphytum officinale)

- **Overview**: Comfrey is a perennial herb known for its bell-shaped flowers and large, hairy leaves. Traditionally used for healing wounds, it's also popular in organic gardening as a fertilizer.

- **Active Compounds**: Allantoin (promotes cell growth), rosmarinic acid, and mucilage.

- **Uses Against Diseases**: Used topically for its anti-inflammatory properties to help heal bruises, sprains, and ulcers. Not recommended for internal use due to the presence of liver-toxic pyrrolizidine alkaloids.

- **Preparation Methods, Dosage, Safety, and Precautions**: Comfrey is often used in ointments, creams, or as a poultice. Only apply to unbroken skin for short periods, and it's not safe for ingestion, pregnant or nursing women, or children.

Coriander (Coriandrum sativum)

- **Overview**: Coriander, or cilantro, is an annual herb with aromatic leaves and seeds, used both as a culinary spice and a medicinal herb.

- **Active Compounds**: Linalool and pinene, which have antioxidant and digestive properties.

- **Uses Against Diseases**: Helps in the management of diabetes by lowering blood sugar levels, improves digestion, and has anti-anxiety effects.

- **Preparation Methods, Dosage, Safety, and Precautions**: Fresh leaves or dried seeds can be used in cooking. As an essential oil, it should be diluted. Generally safe in culinary amounts, large medicinal doses should be avoided during pregnancy.

Cranberry (Vaccinium macrocarpon)

- **Overview**: Cranberry is a small, evergreen shrub known for its tart red berries, primarily grown in North America.

- **Active Compounds**: Proanthocyanidins, which prevent bacteria from adhering to the urinary tract walls.

- **Uses Against Diseases**: Primarily used to prevent and treat urinary tract infections (UTIs). Also has potential benefits for cardiovascular health and gastric ulcer prevention.

- **Preparation Methods, Dosage, Safety, and Precautions**: Consumed as juice, extract, or in capsule form. Typically safe when used in moderate amounts, though excessive consumption can cause stomach upset or increase the risk of kidney stones. Unsweetened juice is preferable as it contains less sugar.

Cubeb Pepper (Piper cubeba)

- **Overview**: Cubeb pepper, also known as Java pepper, is a plant in the pepper family native to Indonesia. It's known for its peppery taste and slightly bitter flavor.

- **Active Compounds**: Essential oils containing monoterpenes and sesquiterpenes, such as sabinene and caryophyllene.

- **Uses Against Diseases**: Traditionally used to treat oral and dental infections, chronic pharyngitis, and sinusitis. Also used as an antiseptic and to ease digestive issues.

- **Preparation Methods, Dosage, Safety, and Precautions**: Can be used in cooking as a spice or taken in extract form. Should be used with caution as large doses can lead to gastrointestinal irritation or kidney damage.

Cumin (Cuminum cyminum)

- **Overview**: Cumin is a flowering plant in the family Apiaceae, native to the Middle East and India. Its seeds are used in many cuisines globally.

- **Active Compounds**: Contains cuminaldehyde, thymol, and phosphorus, which aid digestion and improve immunity.

- **Uses Against Diseases**: Promotes digestion, improves immunity, and may help in treating respiratory disorders like asthma and bronchitis. Cumin is also noted for its anti-carcinogenic properties.

- **Preparation Methods, Dosage, Safety, and Precautions**: Typically used as a spice in cooking. Cumin oil should be used with care as it can cause liver and kidney damage if consumed in large amounts. Generally safe in food quantities, and there are no specific precautions for pregnant or nursing women, though moderation is advised.

Curry Leaf (Murraya koenigii)

- **Overview**: Curry leaf is a tropical to sub-tropical tree in the Rutaceae family, native to India and Sri Lanka, known for its aromatic leaves.

- **Active Compounds**: Contains carbazole alkaloids which have antioxidant properties.

- **Uses Against Diseases**: Used to combat indigestion, diabetes, and to improve eyesight. Also believed to have anti-cancer properties.

- **Preparation Methods, Dosage, Safety, and Precautions**: Often used fresh in cooking or dried and powdered. Generally considered safe in culinary amounts, but the safety of medicinal doses hasn't been established, so consult a healthcare provider.

Dandelion (Taraxacum officinale)

- **Overview**: Commonly regarded as a weed, dandelion is a nutritious plant with high vitamin and mineral content, including iron, calcium, and potassium.

- **Active Compounds**: Contains taraxacin, taraxasterol, and inulin.

- **Uses Against Diseases**: Used to support liver health, detoxification, and has anti-inflammatory effects. Also used as a diuretic.

- **Preparation Methods, Dosage, Safety, and Precautions**: Leaves, roots, and flowers can be used in teas, capsules, or extracts. Generally safe, but some people may experience allergic reactions or contact dermatitis.

Deer Antler Velvet (Cervus elaphus linnaeus)

- **Overview**: Refers to the soft, newly grown antler tissue which is harvested for use in supplements.

- **Active Compounds**: Contains IGF-1, collagen, and various minerals.

- **Uses Against Diseases**: Used in traditional medicine to support joint health, boost strength and endurance, and improve immune function.

- **Preparation Methods, Dosage, Safety, and Precautions**: Available in powder or capsule form. The safety profile is not well-established and can interact with several medications. It's banned in professional sports due to IGF-1 content.

Devil's Claw (Harpagophytum procumbens)

- **Overview**: Native to southern Africa, named for the appearance of its fruit, which is covered in hooks.

- **Active Compounds**: Harpagoside and harpagide, which have anti-inflammatory properties.

- **Uses Against Diseases**: Primarily used for relieving joint pain, arthritis, and back pain.

- **Preparation Methods, Dosage, Safety, and Precautions**: Typically taken in capsules or as a tea. Should be avoided by pregnant women and those with ulcers or gallstones.

Dittany of Crete (Origanum dictamnus)

- **Overview**: A perennial plant native to Crete, known for its healing properties and aromatic leaves.

- **Active Compounds**: Rich in phenolic compounds, including carvacrol, thymol, and flavonoids.

- **Uses Against Diseases**: Used for its antiseptic, antifungal, and anti-inflammatory effects. Traditionally used for wound healing and stomach ailments.

- **Preparation Methods, Dosage, Safety, and Precautions**: Often used as an herb in cooking or as a tea. Generally considered safe in typical culinary or herbal tea amounts.

Dong Quai (Angelica sinensis)

- **Overview**: Often called "female ginseng," Dong Quai is a traditional Chinese herb used to support women's health.

- **Active Compounds**: Contains phytoestrogens, coumarins, and ferulic acid.

- **Uses Against Diseases**: Used to ease menstrual cramps, manage menopausal symptoms, and improve circulation.

- **Preparation Methods, Dosage, Safety, and Precautions**: Available in tinctures, powders, and capsules. It should be avoided during pregnancy due to its potential to stimulate the uterus and should be used cautiously by those with bleeding disorders or hormone-sensitive conditions.

Dragon's Blood (Croton lechleri)

- **Overview**: A bright red resin obtained from various species of a number of distinct plant genera: Croton, Dracaena, Daemonorops, Calamus rotang and Pterocarpus.

- **Active Compounds**: Contains taspine, a cicatrizant (wound-healing) agent, and proanthocyanidins, which are antioxidants.

- **Uses Against Diseases**: Used topically for its healing properties on wounds, ulcers, and for treating gastrointestinal issues when taken internally.

- **Preparation Methods, Dosage, Safety, and Precautions**: Typically applied topically as a liquid or ointment. Internal use should be done cautiously due to potential digestive system irritation. Always ensure it's diluted if used internally.

Echinacea (Echinacea purpurea)

- **Overview**: Native to North America, echinacea is widely used to prevent or treat the common cold.

- **Active Compounds**: Contains alkamides, which can boost immune health, and polysaccharides, known to have immune-enhancing effects.

- **Uses Against Diseases**: Commonly used to reduce the symptoms and duration of the common cold and flu. Also has anti-inflammatory properties.

- **Preparation Methods, Dosage, Safety, and Precautions**: Available in teas, capsules, tinctures, and extracts. Generally considered safe for short-term use, although it can cause allergic reactions in people sensitive to the Asteraceae/Compositae family.

Elderberry (Sambucus nigra)

- **Overview**: A plant native to Europe, North America, and parts of Asia, known for its dark berries and flowers which are both used medicinally.

- **Active Compounds**: Rich in anthocyanins which have antioxidant properties.

- **Uses Against Diseases**: Used for its antiviral properties especially against the flu and common cold, and for immune system boosting.

- **Preparation Methods, Dosage, Safety, and Precautions**: Consumed as syrups, lozenges, capsules, and teas. Raw berries should not be eaten as they are toxic; only cooked berries are safe to consume. Generally safe when used properly, but care should be taken by pregnant women and those on diuretic medications.

Epimedium (Epimedium grandiflorum)

- **Overview**: Commonly known as "horny goat weed," it's a flowering plant native to China known for its aphrodisiac properties.

- **Active Compounds**: Contains icariin, which has been shown to have effects on improving sexual function and osteoporosis.

- **Uses Against Diseases**: Used to enhance libido, treat erectile dysfunction, and support bone health.

- **Preparation Methods, Dosage, Safety, and Precautions**: Available in capsules, tablets, and teas. Should be used with caution as it may interact with various medications and has potential hormone-like effects. Not recommended for long-term use without professional guidance.

Eucalyptus (Eucalyptus globulus)

- **Overview**: Native to Australia, eucalyptus is well-known for its pungent leaves that are rich in medicinal oils.

- **Active Compounds**: Mainly cineole, which has potent antiseptic and decongestant properties.

- **Uses Against Diseases**: Widely used to alleviate symptoms of coughs, colds, and respiratory congestion; also applied topically for its antimicrobial properties.

- **Preparation Methods, Dosage, Safety, and Precautions**: Often used in inhalants, cough syrups, and topical ointments. Pure essential oil should be used cautiously—never ingested and always diluted when applied to the skin to prevent irritation.

Eucalyptus Leaf (Eucalyptus globulus)

- **Overview**: The leaves of the eucalyptus tree are used for their concentrated essential oils.

- **Active Compounds**: Contains high levels of antioxidants, flavonoids, and tannins, which contribute to its anti-inflammatory effects.

- **Uses Against Diseases**: Primarily used for treating respiratory issues such as bronchitis and sinusitis.

- **Preparation Methods, Dosage, Safety, and Precautions**: Can be brewed into a tea or used as an inhalant. It is important to handle with care to avoid digestive upset and allergic reactions.

Evening Primrose (Oenothera biennis)

- **Overview**: This plant's yellow flowers bloom in the evening and it is valued for its seeds that are high in fatty acids.

- **Active Compounds**: Rich in gamma-linolenic acid (GLA), an important omega-6 fatty acid.

- **Uses Against Diseases**: Used to manage eczema, rheumatoid arthritis, and symptoms of PMS and menopause.

- **Preparation Methods, Dosage, Safety, and Precautions**: The oil extracted from the seeds is available in capsules. It's generally safe, but should be avoided by those taking blood thinners and pregnant women due to potential complications.

Fenugreek (Trigonella foenum-graecum)

- **Overview**: An herb native to the Mediterranean, used both as a spice and a supplement.

- **Active Compounds**: Rich in saponins and fibers, with notable amounts of diosgenin, which mimics estrogen.

- **Uses Against Diseases**: Known to enhance lactation, stabilize blood sugar, reduce cholesterol, and aid digestion.

- **Preparation Methods, Dosage, Safety, and Precautions**: Available as whole seeds, powder, or capsules. Generally safe in culinary and medicinal amounts, though it can interact with blood sugar medications and should be used cautiously by pregnant women due to its potential hormonal effects.

Fenugreek Seed (Trigonella foenum-graecum)

- **Overview**: Concentrating on the seeds, which are used more intensively for their health benefits than the leaves.

- **Active Compounds**: High in dietary fiber, saponins, and diosgenin, contributing to its anti-inflammatory and glucose-regulation properties.

- **Uses Against Diseases**: Specifically utilized for its anti-inflammatory properties and its ability to help manage diabetes.

- **Preparation Methods, Dosage, Safety, and Precautions**: Used similarly to the whole plant but with a focus on managing blood sugar levels and reducing inflammation. Safe in typical dietary amounts, though the same precautions apply regarding diabetes medications and pregnancy.

Fingerroot (Boesenbergia rotunda)

- **Overview**: Known also as Chinese ginger, fingerroot is a culinary and medicinal herb from Southeast Asia.

- **Active Compounds**: Contains essential oils and flavonoids that exhibit antioxidant and anti-inflammatory properties.

- **Uses Against Diseases**: Commonly used to improve digestion, relieve flatulence, and as an aphrodisiac. Also investigated for its potential in combating cancer cells.

- **Preparation Methods, Dosage, Safety, and Precautions**: Used as a spice in cooking and can be taken as an extract or powder supplement. Generally safe when consumed in food amounts, but the safety of medicinal doses is not well-documented.

Fireweed (Chamerion angustifolium)

- **Overview**: Fireweed is a perennial herb with a long history of use in native American and traditional European medicine.

- **Active Compounds**: Rich in vitamins A and C, and contains flavonoids and tannins which provide its anti-inflammatory properties.

- **Uses Against Diseases**: Traditionally used to treat inflammation of the urinary tract, prostate disorders, and various skin conditions.

- **Preparation Methods, Dosage, Safety, and Precautions**: Can be consumed as tea made from the leaves and flowers. Generally safe when used appropriately, but specific dose recommendations and long-term safety studies are lacking.

Flaxseed (Linum usitatissimum)

- **Overview**: Flaxseed is known for being a rich source of dietary fiber, omega-3 fatty acids, and lignans.

- **Active Compounds**: High in alpha-linolenic acid, fiber, and lignans that have antioxidant and estrogen properties.

- **Uses Against Diseases**: Used to improve cardiovascular health, aid digestion, and potentially reduce the risk of cancer. Also beneficial for menopausal symptoms.

- **Preparation Methods, Dosage, Safety, and Precautions**: Available as whole seeds, ground meal, or oil. Generally safe in food amounts; however, large doses can cause bowel obstruction, and flaxseed oil should not be cooked at high temperatures due to its low smoke point. Pregnant and breastfeeding women should consult a healthcare provider before starting high-dose supplementation.

Frankincense (Boswellia sacra)

- **Overview**: Frankincense is a resin derived from the Boswellia tree, historically valued for its aromatic and medicinal properties.

- **Active Compounds**: Contains boswellic acids, which have anti-inflammatory and analgesic properties.

- **Uses Against Diseases**: Used for its anti-inflammatory effects in conditions like arthritis, asthma, and various inflammatory bowel diseases.

- **Preparation Methods, Dosage, Safety, and Precautions**: Available in resin, oil, and capsule forms. Generally safe when used as directed, but it can interact with medications and may cause stomach upset in some people.

Fennel (Foeniculum vulgare)

- **Overview**: Fennel is a flavorful, medicinal herb that resembles celery with lacy fronds and a bulbous base.

- **Active Compounds**: Rich in anethole, which has antispasmodic and anti-inflammatory properties.

- **Uses Against Diseases**: Commonly used to treat digestive problems such as bloating, gas, and colic in infants. Also used to improve women's health, particularly in regulating menstrual cycles.

- **Preparation Methods, Dosage, Safety, and Precautions**: Can be used as seeds, oil, or tea. Generally safe when used in food amounts, but high doses of the oil should be avoided, especially by pregnant women, as it can affect estrogen levels.

Garlic (Allium sativum)

- **Overview**: Garlic is well-known for its characteristic pungent flavor and health-promoting properties.

- **Active Compounds**: Contains allicin, which has antibacterial and antifungal properties, along with other sulfur-containing compounds that have various health benefits.

- **Uses Against Diseases**: Widely used to boost the immune system, reduce blood pressure and cholesterol levels, and protect against heart disease. Also has anticancer properties.

- **Preparation Methods, Dosage, Safety, and Precautions**: Can be eaten raw or cooked, taken as capsules, or applied topically as oil. Raw garlic can cause gastrointestinal upset in some people and should be used with caution by those taking blood thinners.

Gentian Root (Gentiana lutea)

- **Overview**: Gentian is a bitter herb that stimulates digestion and improves gastrointestinal function.

- **Active Compounds**: Contains bitter glycosides such as gentiopicrin, which stimulate digestive enzymes and increase bile flow.

- **Uses Against Diseases**: Used to treat indigestion, heartburn, and flatulence. Also used in herbal bitters to promote appetite and digestion.

- **Preparation Methods, Dosage, Safety, and Precautions**: Typically consumed as a tea, tincture, or in digestive bitters. Should be avoided by those with stomach ulcers, high blood pressure, or pregnancy due to its strong stimulatory effects on the digestive system.

Goldenseal (Hydrastis canadensis)

- **Overview**: Goldenseal is a small plant with a yellow root that is highly valued in herbal medicine.

- **Active Compounds**: Contains alkaloids such as berberine, hydrastine, and canadine, which have antimicrobial and anti-inflammatory properties.

- **Uses Against Diseases**: Traditionally used to treat skin disorders, digestive issues, and as a topical antimicrobial. Also used to enhance the medicinal effects of other herbs.

- **Preparation Methods, Dosage, Safety, and Precautions**: Available in tinctures, capsules, and topical preparations. Due to its strong effects, it should be used in moderation; long-term use is not recommended as it can disrupt normal flora and interfere with vitamin B absorption.

Hemp (Cannabis sativa)

- **Overview**: Hemp seeds and oil are used for their nutritional benefits, rich in fatty acids, protein, and fiber.

- **Active Compounds**: High in essential fatty acids like omega-3 and omega-6, gamma-linolenic acid, and a range of amino acids.

- **Uses Against Diseases**: Known for improving skin conditions (such as eczema), reducing inflammation, and supporting heart health.

- **Preparation Methods, Dosage, Safety, and Precautions**: Consumed as seeds, oil, protein powder, or milk. Hemp is generally safe and does not contain THC (the psychoactive component of cannabis) at levels that cause intoxication. However, its consumption should be checked if there are specific dietary restrictions or allergies.

Hibiscus (Hibiscus sabdariffa)

- **Overview**: Often consumed as a tea, hibiscus flowers are known for their bright red color and tart flavor.

- **Active Compounds**: Rich in vitamin C, minerals, and antioxidants, particularly anthocyanins which give it its deep red color.

- **Uses Against Diseases**: Has potential benefits in lowering blood pressure, reducing blood sugar levels, and has diuretic properties which can help in weight management.

- **Preparation Methods, Dosage, Safety, and Precautions**: Typically consumed as a tea. It is safe for most people in moderate amounts, though it can lower blood pressure significantly in some cases and might interact with certain medications.

Holy Basil (Ocimum sanctum)

- **Overview**: Holy basil, also known as Tulsi, is a sacred herb in Indian culture and Ayurvedic medicine.

- **Active Compounds**: Contains eugenol, ursolic acid, and rosmarinic acid, which provide adaptogenic, anti-inflammatory, and antioxidant properties.

- **Uses Against Diseases**: Used to enhance stress response and increase resilience, support immune health, and reduce blood sugar levels. Also has potential benefits in improving asthma and balancing cholesterol.

- **Preparation Methods, Dosage, Safety, and Precautions**: Commonly consumed as tea or supplement. Generally safe when used in food amounts, but as a medicinal herb, it should be used under supervision to avoid potential interactions with medications, especially blood thinners and drugs that lower blood sugar.

Horseradish (Armoracia rusticana)

- **Overview**: Horseradish is a pungent root vegetable used both as a food and for its medicinal properties.

- **Active Compounds**: Contains glucosinolates, which are thought to have antimicrobial and cancer-preventive properties.

- **Uses Against Diseases**: Traditionally used to treat urinary tract infections and sinus infections, and as a stimulant to improve circulation.

- **Preparation Methods, Dosage, Safety, and Precautions**: Commonly grated fresh as a condiment. Should be used with caution in medicinal amounts as it can cause irritation to the stomach and mucous membranes.

Horsetail (Equisetum arvense)

- **Overview**: Known for its high silica content, horsetail is used to promote bone and tissue health.

- **Active Compounds**: Rich in silica, which is crucial for healthy skin, hair, and nails, as well as having diuretic properties.

- **Uses Against Diseases**: Traditionally used to strengthen bones, improve skin health, and for urinary and renal health.

- **Preparation Methods, Dosage, Safety, and Precautions**: Consumed as tea or in capsules. It is generally safe in moderate amounts but should be avoided by those with kidney issues or using diuretics due to its potential to cause electrolyte imbalances.

Hyssop (Hyssopus officinalis)

- **Overview**: Hyssop is a perennial herb with a long history of use in medicine and cooking.

- **Active Compounds**: Contains volatile oils, flavonoids, and other compounds that contribute to its antiseptic, antiviral, and expectorant properties.

- **Uses Against Diseases**: Used to treat respiratory conditions, aid digestion, and as a nerve tonic. Also applied topically for skin infections and wounds.

- **Preparation Methods, Dosage, Safety, and Precautions**: Can be used as a tea, tincture, or essential oil. Not recommended for use in people with epilepsy or during pregnancy due to its high thujone content, which can cause convulsions.

Jasmine (Jasminum officinale)

- **Overview**: Jasmine is prized for its highly fragrant flowers, used both for their pleasant scent and medicinal properties.

- **Active Compounds**: Contains linalool and other components that may help relax the nervous system.

- **Uses Against Diseases**: Often used in aromatherapy to promote relaxation and reduce stress. Its oil is also used for skin care due to its moisturizing and potentially anti-inflammatory properties.

- **Preparation Methods, Dosage, Safety, and Precautions**: Commonly used in the form of tea or essential oil. Jasmine tea is safe for most people in moderate amounts, but the essential oil should be diluted before topical application to avoid irritation.

Juniper (Juniperus communis)

- **Overview**: Juniper berries, the female seed cone produced by various species of junipers, are not true berries but cone-like structures. Known for their distinctive aroma, they are commonly used in culinary applications and traditional medicine.

- **Active Compounds**: Contains volatile oils, including sabinene, limonene, and pinene, which have diuretic, antiseptic, and anti-inflammatory properties.

- **Uses Against Diseases**: Traditionally used to treat urinary tract infections, digestive problems, and relieve arthritis pain. Also noted for its potential to support heart health and improve skin conditions.

- **Preparation Methods, Dosage, Safety, and Precautions**: Often used in cooking, teas, or as essential oil. When using medicinally, it should not be consumed in large quantities or for prolonged periods as it can cause kidney irritation. Not recommended for pregnant women due to potential uterine stimulation.

Kava (Piper methysticum)

- **Overview**: Kava is a plant native to the Pacific Islands, where it has been used for centuries as a ceremonial drink to promote relaxation.

- **Active Compounds**: Kavalactones are the primary active components, known for their psychoactive properties that can reduce anxiety and promote relaxation without impairing cognitive function.

- **Uses Against Diseases**: Widely used for its anxiolytic (anti-anxiety) effects. Also used to aid sleep and as a muscle relaxant.

- **Preparation Methods, Dosage, Safety, and Precautions**: Typically consumed as a drink made from the root, or as capsules and tinctures. While effective for anxiety, its safety is debated due to reports of liver toxicity associated with its use. It should not be used with alcohol or other medications that affect the liver.

Lavender (Lavandula angustifolia)

- **Overview**: Lavender is famed for its fragrance and is used extensively in aromatherapy, cosmetics, and medicine.

- **Active Compounds**: Contains linalool and linalyl acetate, which are believed to help promote relaxation and calm nerves.

- **Uses Against Diseases**: Commonly used to alleviate anxiety, stress, and insomnia. Also used topically for its antiseptic and anti-inflammatory properties to treat minor burns and bug bites.

- **Preparation Methods, Dosage, Safety, and Precautions**: Can be used in essential oil form, in teas, or as extracts. Essential oil should be diluted before topical application or inhalation. Generally considered safe, but oral ingestion of the oil should be avoided unless under the supervision of a health professional.

Lemon Balm (Melissa officinalis)

- **Overview**: Lemon balm, a member of the mint family, is noted for its lemon-scented leaves.

- **Active Compounds**: Contains rosmarinic acid, terpenes, and tannins, which have antiviral, antimicrobial, and calming properties.

- **Uses Against Diseases**: Used for reducing stress and anxiety, promoting sleep, improving appetite, and easing pain and discomfort from indigestion.

- **Preparation Methods, Dosage, Safety, and Precautions**: Commonly consumed as tea or in extracts and tinctures. Generally safe when used in typical culinary or therapeutic amounts, though excessive consumption can lead to sedative effects and should be avoided during pregnancy and breastfeeding without medical supervision.

Lavandin (Lavandula x intermedia)

- **Overview**: Lavandin is a hybrid of true lavender and spike lavender, known for its robust fragrance and higher oil content.

- **Active Compounds**: Contains linalool, camphor, and terpineol, which contribute to its aromatic and therapeutic properties.

- **Uses Against Diseases**: Commonly used in aromatherapy for stress relief and relaxation. Also has antiseptic and anti-inflammatory properties, making it useful in treating minor cuts, burns, and skin irritations.

- **Preparation Methods, Dosage, Safety, and Precautions**: Often used in the form of essential oil in diffusers, soaps, and lotions. Essential oil should always be diluted before topical application to prevent irritation.

Lemon Grass (Cymbopogon citratus)

- **Overview**: Lemon grass is a tropical plant known for its strong lemon scent and flavor, widely used in culinary and medicinal practices.

- **Active Compounds**: Contains citral, which has anti-inflammatory and antimicrobial properties.

- **Uses Against Diseases**: Used to relieve pain, reduce fever, improve digestive function, and as an insect repellent. Also has calming effects that may help reduce stress and improve sleep.

- **Preparation Methods, Dosage, Safety, and Precautions**: Can be consumed as tea, used in cooking, or applied topically as an essential oil. Should be consumed with caution in medicinal amounts as it can lead to stomach irritation and should be avoided during pregnancy.

Lemon Verbena (Aloysia citrodora)

- **Overview**: Lemon verbena is appreciated for its intense lemony fragrance, used both in culinary applications and traditional medicine.

- **Active Compounds**: Contains verbascoside, which has antioxidant and anti-inflammatory properties.

- **Uses Against Diseases**: Used to reduce inflammation, aid in digestion, and promote relaxation. Also used for its potential weight loss benefits.

- **Preparation Methods, Dosage, Safety, and Precautions**: Typically used as a tea or in extract form. Generally safe when used in moderation, but high doses can cause skin sensitization when exposed to sunlight and gastrointestinal issues.

Licorice Root (Glycyrrhiza glabra)

- **Overview**: Licorice root is widely used in herbal medicine for its numerous health benefits, distinct from the similar-sounding licorice used for flavoring sweets.

- **Active Compounds**: Contains glycyrrhizin, which has potent anti-inflammatory and immune-boosting properties.

- **Uses Against Diseases**: Used to treat peptic ulcers, respiratory problems, and liver conditions. Also has applications in treating adrenal insufficiency.

- **Preparation Methods, Dosage, Safety, and Precautions**: Available as dried root, tea, extract, or powder. Overconsumption can lead to serious side effects, including hypertension, low potassium levels, and fluid retention, especially when consumed in large amounts over an extended period.

Marigold (Calendula officinalis)

- **Overview**: Not to be confused with the ornamental marigold, Calendula is used for its healing properties.

- **Active Compounds**: Contains triterpenoids, flavonoids, and carotenoids that contribute to its anti-inflammatory and healing effects.

- **Uses Against Diseases**: Commonly used topically to heal wounds, burns, and rashes. It's also used to reduce inflammation and treat sore throat when taken orally.

- **Preparation Methods, Dosage, Safety, and Precautions**: Available as creams, oils, or teas. Generally safe when used topically; however, those with allergies to plants in the Asteraceae family should avoid calendula.

Marshmallow (Althaea officinalis)

- **Overview**: The root and leaves of marshmallow plant are used for their mucilage content, which soothes mucous membranes.

- **Active Compounds**: High mucilage content along with pectin and flavonoids that provide anti-inflammatory and immunomodulatory effects.

- **Uses Against Diseases**: Traditionally used to soothe respiratory and digestive tracts. Effective against cough, sore throat, and digestive issues like ulcers and indigestion.

- **Preparation Methods, Dosage, Safety, and Precautions**: Can be consumed as tea or used in extracts. Marshmallow is generally safe, but due to its mucilage content, it may interfere with the absorption of other medications.

Mint (Mentha spicata)

- **Overview**: Mint, known for its aromatic leaves, is widely used in both culinary and medicinal applications.

- **Active Compounds**: Contains menthol, which provides its cooling sensation, along with various antioxidants.

- **Uses Against Diseases**: Commonly used to aid digestion, relieve nausea, and alleviate symptoms of irritable bowel syndrome (IBS). Also used for its calming effects on the respiratory tract.

- **Preparation Methods, Dosage, Safety, and Precautions**: Can be consumed as tea, added to foods, or inhaled through essential oils. Generally safe in food and medicinal amounts, though excessive consumption can cause heartburn or allergic reactions.

Mugwort (Artemisia vulgaris)

- **Overview**: Mugwort is a plant with a long history of use in traditional medicine, especially in Europe and Asia, for its digestive and calming effects.

- **Active Compounds**: Contains thujone, flavonoids, and coumarin derivatives.

- **Uses Against Diseases**: Often used to stimulate the appetite, ease digestion, and promote menstrual flow. Also used in moxibustion in traditional Chinese medicine.

- **Preparation Methods, Dosage, Safety, and Precautions**: Can be consumed as tea or used in dried form for smoking or moxibustion. Should be avoided during pregnancy and by those with allergy to ragweed and related plants.

Nettle (Urtica dioica)

- **Overview**: Nettle is valued for its nutrient-rich leaves and has been used as a food and medicine throughout history.

- **Active Compounds**: Rich in vitamins A, C, and K, as well as iron and several antioxidants.

- **Uses Against Diseases**: Used to treat arthritis, anemia, and urinary tract infections. Also known for its anti-inflammatory effects and ability to support prostate health.

- **Preparation Methods, Dosage, Safety, and Precautions**: Can be consumed as tea, in soups, or as a cooked green. Fresh nettle can cause skin irritation when handled, so gloves are recommended during preparation.

Oat Straw (Avena sativa)

- **Overview**: Oat straw comes from the green stalks of the oat plant before it reaches full maturity, known for its nutritional and therapeutic benefits.

- **Active Compounds**: Rich in silica, magnesium, phosphorus, chromium, iron, calcium, alkaloids, protein, the B-complex vitamins, and vitamins A and C.

- **Uses Against Diseases**: Used to support nervous system health, improve mood, reduce inflammation, and enhance bone health. Also believed to help in managing cholesterol levels and improving heart health.

- **Preparation Methods, Dosage, Safety, and Precautions**: Typically consumed as tea or in capsule form. Generally safe for most people, but it's important to ensure gluten-free sources for those with celiac disease or gluten intolerance.

Olive Leaf (Olea europaea)

- **Overview**: Extracted from the leaves of the olive tree, olive leaf has been used medicinally in various cultures, particularly in Mediterranean regions.

- **Active Compounds**: Contains oleuropein, which has antioxidant, anti-inflammatory, antibacterial, and antiviral properties.

- **Uses Against Diseases**: Used to enhance immune system response, reduce blood pressure, manage diabetes, and improve cardiovascular health.

- **Preparation Methods, Dosage, Safety, and Precautions**: Available as capsules, extracts, or teas. Generally well-tolerated but can cause mild side effects such as headache or dizziness in some cases.

Oregano (Origanum vulgare)

- **Overview**: Oregano is a common culinary herb also known for its potent medicinal properties.

- **Active Compounds**: Contains thymol and carvacrol, which have strong antibacterial and antifungal effects.

- **Uses Against Diseases**: Used to treat respiratory tract disorders, gastrointestinal (GI) disorders, menstrual cramps, and urinary tract disorders. Also applied topically to help treat a number of skin conditions, including acne and dandruff.

- **Preparation Methods, Dosage, Safety, and Precautions**: Can be used fresh or dried in culinary applications, as well as in oil form. Oregano oil should be diluted before topical application or ingestion due to its potency. It may cause stomach upset in high doses.

Parsley (Petroselinum crispum)

- **Overview**: Commonly used as a garnish, parsley is a nutrient-rich herb.

- **Active Compounds**: Rich in vitamins A, C, and K, and contains antioxidants such as flavonoids, luteolin, and apigenin.

- **Uses Against Diseases**: Promotes kidney health and diuresis, helps in controlling blood pressure, and supports bone health due to its high vitamin K content.

- **Preparation Methods, Dosage, Safety, and Precautions**: Can be consumed fresh in salads, as a juice, or as a tea. Generally safe in food amounts, but large medicinal amounts should be avoided during pregnancy as it can influence uterine contractions.

Passionflower (Passiflora incarnata)

- **Overview**: Known for its beautiful flowers and medicinal uses, passionflower is used primarily for its calming and sedative effects.

- **Active Compounds**: Contains flavonoids such as vitexin and isovitexin, which are believed to contribute to its soothing effects on the central nervous system.

- **Uses Against Diseases**: Used to treat anxiety, insomnia, and certain forms of neuralgia. Also used for its antispasmodic effects on digestive issues like indigestion and nausea.

- **Preparation Methods, Dosage, Safety, and Precautions**: Available in teas, extracts, and tablets. Generally considered safe, but may cause drowsiness. Should be used with caution when driving or operating machinery and should not be combined with sedative medications.

Peppermint (Mentha piperita)

- **Overview**: Peppermint is a popular herb known for its refreshing aroma and cooling effect, commonly used in food, cosmetics, and medicine.

- **Active Compounds**: Contains menthol, which provides its characteristic cooling sensation and has antispasmodic properties.

- **Uses Against Diseases**: Widely used to relieve symptoms of irritable bowel syndrome (IBS), nausea, and other digestive issues. Also effective as a decongestant and analgesic.

- **Preparation Methods, Dosage, Safety, and Precautions**: Can be consumed as tea, capsules, or essential oil. The oil should be diluted if applied topically or used aromatically. Should not be applied to the face of infants or small children due to the risk of respiratory distress.

Red Clover (Trifolium pratense)

- **Overview**: Red clover is a perennial herb with pinkish-purple flowers, used traditionally in various cultures for its health properties.

- **Active Compounds**: Contains isoflavones, which have estrogen-like properties and may help balance hormones.

- **Uses Against Diseases**: Often used to ease menopausal symptoms such as hot flashes and night sweats. Also used for skin health and as a detoxifying herb.

- **Preparation Methods, Dosage, Safety, and Precautions**: Available in teas, tinctures, and capsules. Should be used with caution in individuals with hormone-sensitive conditions or those taking hormone therapy.

Rose (Rosa spp.)

- **Overview**: Rose petals are used for their fragrant properties in culinary and cosmetic applications, and have medicinal benefits as well.

- **Active Compounds**: Contains essential oils, vitamin C, polyphenols, and other antioxidants.

- **Uses Against Diseases**: Often used for its calming and antidepressant effects. Also applied topically to improve skin health and to treat minor abrasions and cuts.

- **Preparation Methods, Dosage, Safety, and Precautions**: Can be used in teas, jellies, syrups, and essential oil form. Generally safe when used appropriately, though the essential oil should be diluted before topical application to prevent irritation.

Rosemary (Rosmarinus officinalis)

- **Overview**: Rosemary is a perennial herb with needle-like leaves, popular in cooking and herbal medicine.

- **Active Compounds**: Contains rosmarinic acid, carnosic acid, and essential oils that have antioxidant, anti-inflammatory, and antimicrobial properties.

- **Uses Against Diseases**: Used to improve memory, support digestion, and relieve muscle pain and spasms. Also thought to support hair growth and scalp health.

- **Preparation Methods, Dosage, Safety, and Precautions**: Often used as a culinary herb, in teas, and as an essential oil. Generally safe in culinary amounts, but high doses of the essential oil can be toxic and should be used with caution.

Sage (Salvia officinalis)

- **Overview**: Sage is a staple herb in various cuisines, also revered for its medicinal properties.

- **Active Compounds**: Contains thujone, camphor, and other volatile oils, as well as flavonoids and phenolic acids.

- **Uses Against Diseases**: Commonly used for its digestive and calming properties. Also has antibacterial qualities and is used in gargles to soothe sore throats.

- **Preparation Methods, Dosage, Safety, and Precautions**: Can be used fresh or dried in culinary dishes, as well as in teas and supplements. Not recommended in medicinal amounts during pregnancy or for individuals with seizure disorders due to thujone content.

St. John's Wort (Hypericum perforatum)

- **Overview**: St. John's Wort is a perennial plant known for its use in treating depression and other mood disorders.

- **Active Compounds**: Contains hypericin and hyperforin, which are believed to have antidepressant and antiviral activities.

- **Uses Against Diseases**: Primarily used to treat mild to moderate depression, anxiety, and seasonal affective disorder. Also has potential antiviral properties.

- **Preparation Methods, Dosage, Safety, and Precautions**: Available in capsules, teas, and tinctures. Can interact with a wide range of medications, including antidepressants, birth control, and blood thinners, and should be used under the guidance of a healthcare provider.

Spirulina (Arthrospira platensis)

- **Overview**: Spirulina is a blue-green algae known for its nutritional content and health benefits.

- **Active Compounds**: Rich in protein, vitamins B1, B2, B3, copper, and iron, and contains phycocyanin, a potent antioxidant.

- **Uses Against Diseases**: Promotes energy, enhances immune function, and has been shown to lower blood sugar and cholesterol levels. It also has potential anti-inflammatory effects.

- **Preparation Methods, Dosage, Safety, and Precautions**: Available as a powder or tablet supplement. Generally safe for most people, but can be contaminated with harmful bacteria or heavy metals if not sourced from a reputable supplier.

Thyme (Thymus vulgaris)

- **Overview**: Thyme is a culinary and medicinal herb known for its strong, earthy flavor and antimicrobial properties.

- **Active Compounds**: Contains thymol and carvacrol, which have antibacterial, antifungal, and antiviral properties.

- **Uses Against Diseases**: Used to treat respiratory conditions like bronchitis and cough, and as a topical antiseptic for infections and minor wounds.

- **Preparation Methods, Dosage, Safety, and Precautions**: Can be used fresh or dried in cooking, and as an essential oil or tea. Thyme oil should be diluted before topical application and is not recommended for ingestion due to potential toxicity.

Turmeric (Curcuma longa)

- **Overview**: Turmeric is a root known for its bright yellow color and is a staple in Indian cuisine and traditional medicine.

- **Active Compounds**: Contains curcumin, which has powerful anti-inflammatory and antioxidant properties.

- **Uses Against Diseases**: Widely used to reduce inflammation, manage pain, and improve liver function. It is also researched for its potential effects on cancer and Alzheimer's disease.

- **Preparation Methods, Dosage, Safety, and Precautions**: Commonly used as a spice in cooking, and available in capsules, extracts, and teas. Generally safe, but high doses can cause gastrointestinal upset and may interact with blood thinners.

Valerian (Valeriana officinalis)

- **Overview**: Valerian is a plant whose root is used primarily for its sedative and anxiolytic effects.

- **Active Compounds**: Contains valepotriates and sesquiterpenes, which are thought to contribute to its sedative properties.

- **Uses Against Diseases**: Commonly used to treat sleep disorders, anxiety, and psychological stress.

- **Preparation Methods, Dosage, Safety, and Precautions**: Available in capsules, teas, and tinctures. Generally considered safe for short-term use, but it can cause drowsiness, dizziness, and, in rare cases, paradoxical reactions such as anxiety and restlessness. Not recommended for long-term use or in combination with alcohol.

Vervain (Verbena officinalis)

- **Overview**: Vervain is a perennial herb known historically across many cultures for its medicinal properties.

- **Active Compounds**: Contains iridoid glycosides, flavonoids, and tannins, which contribute to its anti-inflammatory and nervine properties.

- **Uses Against Diseases**: Used traditionally to treat anxiety, insomnia, and mild depressive symptoms. Also used for digestive disorders and to alleviate pain from kidney stones and headaches.

- **Preparation Methods, Dosage, Safety, and Precautions**: Typically consumed as a tea or tincture. Generally safe when used in moderation, but can potentially interact with sedative medications and is not recommended during pregnancy due to its uterine stimulant effects.

Vanilla (Vanilla planifolia)

- **Overview**: Vanilla, derived from orchids of the genus Vanilla, is highly prized for its fragrance and flavor, often used in culinary, cosmetic, and aromatherapy applications.

- **Active Compounds**: Contains vanillin, which has antioxidant properties.

- **Uses Against Diseases**: While primarily used for flavoring, vanilla also has mild anti-inflammatory properties that can help soothe and calm in aromatherapy.

- **Preparation Methods, Dosage, Safety, and Precautions**: Commonly used as an extract or as vanilla bean pods in cooking. Vanilla is generally safe for most people when used in food amounts; however, synthetic vanilla or high concentrations of extract should be used cautiously as they can cause headaches or allergic reactions.

Wormwood (Artemisia absinthium)

- **Overview**: Wormwood is best known as the key ingredient in absinthe, a once-banned alcoholic beverage. It has been used traditionally for its digestive and vermifuge properties.

- **Active Compounds**: Contains thujone, which is toxic in high doses, and sesquiterpene lactones, which help stimulate digestion and relieve spasms.

- **Uses Against Diseases**: Used to treat digestive disorders, liver problems, and worm infestations. Also employed in modern herbal bitters and tonics to improve appetite and digestion.

- **Preparation Methods, Dosage, Safety, and Precautions**: Typically used in tinctures or as an infusion. High concentrations of thujone in wormwood can be neurotoxic and should be used with caution. Not recommended for prolonged use or in high doses due to potential toxicity.

Yucca (Yucca schidigera)

- **Overview**: Yucca is a plant native to the deserts of North America, known for its ornamental and medicinal uses.

- **Active Compounds**: Contains saponins, which have anti-inflammatory and antioxidant properties.

- **Uses Against Diseases**: Used to treat arthritis and joint pain due to its anti-inflammatory effects. Also believed to promote blood purification and improve overall health.

- **Preparation Methods, Dosage, Safety, and Precautions**: Available in capsules, powders, and extracts. Generally safe when used as directed, but excessive consumption can lead to stomach irritation and other digestive issues.

Ziziphus (Ziziphus jujuba)

- **Overview**: Commonly known as jujube or red date, Ziziphus is a fruit tree native to Asia, valued for its nutritious fruit and medicinal properties.

- **Active Compounds**: Contains high levels of vitamin C, flavonoids, saponins, and polysaccharides, which offer antioxidant, immune-boosting, and sedative effects.

- **Uses Against Diseases**: Used to improve sleep, alleviate anxiety, and as a general tonic to strengthen the body. Also used for its anti-inflammatory and hepatoprotective properties.

- **Preparation Methods, Dosage, Safety, and Precautions**: The fruit can be eaten fresh, dried, or as an extract. Generally safe when consumed in dietary amounts, but care should be taken when using extracts or supplements due to potential interactions with other medications.

Zucchini (Cucurbita pepo)

- **Overview**: Zucchini is a summer squash that is easy to cultivate and rich in vitamins and minerals.

- **Active Compounds**: High in dietary fiber, antioxidants, vitamin C, and potassium.

- **Uses Against Diseases**: Supports cardiovascular health, aids in weight management, and promotes healthy digestion. Its antioxidant properties may also help in reducing oxidative stress.

- **Preparation Methods, Dosage, Safety, and Precautions**: Commonly eaten cooked or raw in a variety of dishes. Generally safe when consumed as part of a regular diet.

Combining Herbs for Maximum Effect

Herbal synergy refers to the amplified effects that arise when combining two or more herbs. This concept is based on the idea that the combined therapeutic benefits of herbs can surpass the effects of each herb used individually. Understanding the unique properties of each herb and how they can work together harmoniously is crucial for achieving optimal health outcomes. By leveraging herbal synergy, you can create more potent and effective remedies that support overall well-being.Benefits of Combining Herbs

1. **Enhanced Efficacy**: Combining herbs can enhance their individual effects, leading to more potent remedies. For instance, pairing ginger with turmeric can amplify their anti-inflammatory properties.

2. **Broadened Therapeutic Range**: A combination of herbs can address multiple symptoms or underlying causes of an ailment, providing a more comprehensive approach to healing.

3. **Reduced Side Effects**: Some herbs can mitigate the side effects of others. For example, combining licorice with peppermint can soothe the stomach while enhancing digestive health.

Principles of Effective Herbal Combinations

1. **Complementary Actions**: Choose herbs with complementary actions to target a specific condition. For instance, Echinacea boosts the immune system, while elderberry has antiviral properties, making them a powerful combination for fighting colds and flu.

2. **Balancing Properties**: Some herbs can balance each other's effects. If one herb is very stimulating, it can be balanced with a calming herb to create a harmonious blend. For example, combining the stimulating effects of ginseng with the calming effects of chamomile can create a balanced energy tonic.

3. **Sequential Use**: Sometimes, it's beneficial to use herbs in a sequence rather than simultaneously. For instance, detoxifying herbs like milk thistle can be used initially to cleanse the liver, followed by nutritive herbs like nettle to rebuild and nourish the body.

Popular Herbal Combinations

1. **Turmeric and Black Pepper**: Turmeric contains curcumin, a powerful anti-inflammatory compound. However, curcumin's bioavailability is low. Black pepper contains piperine, which can enhance the absorption of curcumin by up to 2000%. This combination is often recommended by Barbara O'Neill for its potent anti-inflammatory and antioxidant effects.

2. **Echinacea and Goldenseal**: Echinacea is renowned for its immune-boosting properties, while goldenseal is a potent antimicrobial. Together, they form a robust defense against infections, particularly those involving the respiratory tract.

3. **Valerian and Hops**: Valerian is known for its sedative properties, making it a popular choice for anxiety and insomnia. Hops, another calming herb, enhances these effects, creating a powerful natural remedy for sleep disorders and stress.

4. **Ginger and Lemon Balm**: Ginger aids digestion and has anti-inflammatory properties, while lemon balm is calming and helps with digestive issues linked to stress. This combination can be particularly effective for gastrointestinal discomfort caused by anxiety.

5. **Ginseng and Astragalus**: Ginseng is a well-known adaptogen that helps the body cope with stress and increases energy levels. Astragalus is another adaptogen that supports the immune system. Together, they enhance physical endurance and resilience to stress.

Practical Applications

1. **Tinctures**: Herbal tinctures are liquid extracts that combine the properties of multiple herbs. They are easy to use and can be taken directly or added to water. For example, a tincture combining Echinacea, elderberry, and goldenseal can be a potent remedy during flu season.

2. **Teas**: Herbal teas are a simple and effective way to combine herbs. A tea made with peppermint, ginger, and fennel can provide comprehensive digestive support, addressing nausea, bloating, and gas.

3. **Capsules and Powders**: For those who prefer a more convenient option, combining powdered herbs in capsules can be effective. For example, a blend of ashwagandha, rhodiola, and holy basil in capsule form can support adrenal health and reduce stress.

4. **Topical Applications**: Herbs can also be combined for topical use. A salve made with calendula, comfrey, and St. John's Wort can be applied to wounds and burns for its healing and anti-inflammatory properties.

Dosage, Safety, and Precautions

When combining herbs, it's crucial to consider the appropriate dosages and potential interactions. Always start with lower doses to monitor how your body responds. Barbara O'Neill advises consulting with a healthcare provider, especially when combining herbs with prescription medications.

- **Dosage**: Follow standard guidelines for individual herbs, but start with half the recommended dose when combining to ensure tolerance.

- **Safety**: Be aware of any contraindications. For example, combining blood-thinning herbs like ginkgo and garlic with anticoagulant medications can increase the risk of bleeding.

- **Precautions**: Pregnant and breastfeeding women, as well as individuals with chronic health conditions, should consult a healthcare professional before using combined herbal remedies.

Combining herbs for maximum effect is a nuanced practice that can significantly enhance the therapeutic benefits of natural remedies. By understanding the principles of herbal synergy and following guidelines for safe and effective combinations, you can create powerful remedies that align with Barbara O'Neill's teachings on holistic health and natural healing. Whether you are addressing a specific health condition or seeking to improve overall well-being, the strategic combination of herbs can provide a comprehensive and effective approach to self-healing.

Integrating Herbs into Daily Life

Embracing Herbal Wellness

Integrating herbs into daily life can be a transformative journey towards holistic health and well-being. Here, we explore practical and effective ways to incorporate herbs into your daily life, ensuring you can harness their full potential for health and vitality.

Starting Your Day with Herbs

1. **Herbal Morning Teas**: Begin your day with a cup of herbal tea. Herbs like ginger, lemon balm, and peppermint can invigorate your senses, boost your metabolism, and prepare your digestive system for the day ahead. Starting with ginger tea for its warming and digestive properties, can be particularly beneficial during colder months.

2. **Herbal Infused Water**: Infuse your water with herbs to enhance hydration and enjoy subtle flavors throughout the day. Add fresh mint leaves, slices of cucumber, or a few sprigs of rosemary to your water bottle. This not only makes hydration more enjoyable but also provides gentle detoxification and digestive support.

3. **Herbal Smoothies**: Incorporate herbs into your morning smoothies. Adding a handful of fresh parsley, a dash of turmeric, or a spoonful of spirulina can significantly boost the nutritional value of your smoothies.

Cooking with Herbs

1. **Flavorful Cooking**: Use herbs to enhance the flavor and nutritional profile of your meals. Fresh herbs like basil, thyme, and cilantro can be added to salads, soups, and main dishes. Dried herbs such as oregano, rosemary, and sage are excellent for seasoning roasted vegetables and meats.

2. **Herbal Oils and Vinegars**: Create your own herbal-infused oils and vinegars. These can be used in cooking, salad dressings, or as a finishing touch to dishes. For example, infusing olive oil with garlic and rosemary can add depth of flavor to your cooking while providing anti-inflammatory benefits.

3. **Herbal Soups and Stews**: Incorporate medicinal herbs into soups and stews. Herbs like astragalus and reishi mushrooms can be added to broths for their immune-boosting properties. Barbara often shares recipes that combine traditional cooking with herbal medicine to support the body's health during the colder months.

Herbal Snacks and Supplements

1. **Herbal Energy Balls**: Make herbal energy balls using a blend of nuts, seeds, dried fruits, and powdered herbs. Ingredients like maca powder, chia seeds, and cacao can create a nutrient-dense snack that supports energy levels and overall health.

2. **Herbal Capsules and Tinctures**: For those who prefer a more convenient form of herbal intake, consider herbal capsules and tinctures. These can be taken as supplements to address specific health concerns. Barbara advises choosing high-quality, organic products to ensure potency and safety.

3. **Herbal Spices**: Use powdered herbs and spices in your cooking. Turmeric, cinnamon, and cayenne pepper are not only flavorful but also have significant health benefits. Adding a pinch of these spices to your meals can help reduce inflammation, regulate blood sugar levels, and improve circulation.

Herbal Self-Care Routines

1. **Herbal Baths**: Enhance your bathing routine with the soothing power of herbs. Adding a sachet of lavender, chamomile, and rose petals to your bath creates a relaxing and aromatic experience. Herbal baths are renowned for their calming effects on the nervous system and their ability to promote restful sleep.
2. **Herbal Skin Care**: Incorporate herbal-infused oils and creams into your skincare regimen. Calendula and chamomile oils are excellent for soothing irritated skin, while aloe vera gel provides hydration and healing. Using natural, plant-based products is essential for maintaining healthy, radiant skin.
3. **Aromatherapy**: Integrate essential oils into your daily life. Diffusing oils like eucalyptus, peppermint, and lemon can purify the air, elevate your mood, and support respiratory health. Aromatherapy is a valuable component of a holistic wellness approach, offering a range of benefits for mind and body.

Herbal Remedies for Common Ailments

1. **Digestive Support**: Maintain a selection of herbal teas such as peppermint, fennel, and ginger to support digestion after meals. These herbs can help alleviate bloating, gas, and indigestion. Prioritizing digestive health is fundamental for overall well-being.

2. **Immune Boosting**: Integrate immune-boosting herbs like echinacea, elderberry, and astragalus into your daily routine, especially during flu season. These can be consumed as teas, tinctures, or supplements to strengthen your body's natural defenses.

3. **Stress and Sleep**: Utilize calming herbs such as valerian, passionflower, and lemon balm to manage stress and improve sleep quality. Drinking a cup of chamomile tea before bed can help relax both mind and body, promoting a restful night's sleep.

Educating Yourself and Others

1. **Learning and Sharing**: Invest time in educating yourself about the herbs you use. Read books, attend workshops, and follow reputable sources to deepen your understanding. Sharing this knowledge with friends and family can inspire them to incorporate herbs into their lives as well.

2. **Growing Your Own Herbs**: Start a small herb garden to ensure a fresh supply of herbs and to connect more deeply with the plants. Growing your own herbs fosters a greater appreciation for natural remedies and promotes self-sufficiency.

3. **Keeping a Herbal Journal**: Keep a journal to document your experiences with various herbs. Record their effects, any side effects, and how they integrate into your daily routine. This practice will help you refine your herbal regimen and determine what works best for your body.

Safety and Precautions

1. **Consulting with Professionals**: Always consult with a healthcare provider before starting any new herbal regimen, especially if you have existing health conditions or are taking medication. Barbara emphasizes the importance of integrating natural remedies with conventional care for a balanced approach.

2. **Understanding Contraindications**: Be aware of any potential interactions between herbs and medications. For instance, St. John's Wort can interfere with certain prescription drugs. Educate yourself about these interactions to use herbs safely and effectively.

3. **Starting Slowly**: When introducing new herbs into your routine, start with small amounts to see how your body responds. This approach minimizes the risk of adverse reactions and allows you to gradually build up to the recommended dosage.

Integrating herbs into daily life is a powerful way to support health and wellness. By incorporating these natural remedies into your routine, you can enjoy the benefits of improved digestion, enhanced immunity, reduced stress, and overall vitality. This chapter provides practical and accessible ways to make herbs a seamless part of your life. Whether through cooking, self-care, or supplementation, the consistent use of herbs can lead to profound and lasting health benefits.

Chapter 3: Detoxification and Cleansing

Key Concepts in Detoxification

1. **The Role of the Liver**: The liver is the body's primary detoxification organ. It filters blood, metabolizes toxins, and converts them into harmless substances that can be excreted. Barbara emphasizes the importance of supporting liver health through diet and lifestyle choices, as a well-functioning liver is crucial for effective detoxification.

2. **Kidney Function**: The kidneys filter waste products from the blood and excrete them through urine. Maintaining kidney health is vital for detoxification. Adequate hydration, balanced electrolytes, and minimizing the intake of toxins are essential strategies.

3. **Digestive Health**: A healthy digestive system ensures the efficient elimination of waste. Barbara often discusses the importance of a diet rich in fiber, probiotics, and prebiotics to support gut health and facilitate detoxification.

4. **Lung and Skin Detoxification**: The lungs expel toxins through breath, while the skin eliminates waste through sweat. Practices like deep breathing exercises, regular physical activity, and sauna sessions can enhance these natural detox pathways.

Signs You May Need Detoxification

- **Persistent Fatigue**: Feeling tired despite adequate rest.

- **Digestive Issues**: Bloating, constipation, or diarrhea.

- **Skin Problems**: Acne, rashes, or other skin conditions.

- **Frequent Infections**: A weakened immune system leading to recurring colds or infections.

- **Mental Fog**: Difficulty concentrating or memory problems.

- **Unexplained Aches and Pains**: Persistent muscle or joint pain.

Recognizing these signs is crucial for timely intervention and supporting the body's natural detox processes.

Effective Detoxification Strategies

1. **Dietary Detoxification**: Adopting a clean, nutrient-dense diet is fundamental to detoxification. Barbara advocates for a plant-based diet rich in fruits, vegetables, whole grains, nuts, and seeds. These foods provide essential vitamins, minerals, antioxidants, and fiber, which support detoxification pathways.

- **Cruciferous Vegetables**: Broccoli, cauliflower, and Brussels sprouts enhance liver detoxification.

- **Leafy Greens**: Spinach, kale, and Swiss chard alkalize the body and provide chlorophyll, which helps detoxify the blood.

- **Citrus Fruits**: Lemons, oranges, and grapefruits are high in vitamin C and stimulate liver function.

2. **Hydration**: Drinking plenty of water is essential for kidney function and flushing out toxins. Barbara emphasizes the importance of staying hydrated with clean, filtered water and incorporating hydrating foods like cucumbers and watermelon.

3. **Herbal Support**: Certain herbs can enhance detoxification: milk thistle, dandelion root, and burdock root for their liver-supporting properties. These herbs can be taken as teas, tinctures, or supplements.

   - **Milk Thistle**: Protects liver cells and supports regeneration.

   - **Dandelion Root**: Acts as a diuretic, promoting kidney function.

   - **Burdock Root**: Purifies the blood and supports liver and kidney health.

4. **Physical Activity**: Engaging in regular physical activity promotes circulation and lymphatic drainage, aiding in the removal of toxins from the body. Activities such as yoga, walking, and strength training are highly beneficial. Additionally, rebounding exercises, which involve bouncing on a mini-trampoline, are particularly effective for stimulating the lymphatic system.

5. **Sweat Therapy**: Sweating through exercise or sauna sessions helps eliminate toxins via the skin. Infrared saunas are especially effective for deep tissue detoxification. Combining sauna sessions with cold showers can further boost circulation and enhance the detoxification process.

6. **Dry Brushing**: This practice involves using a natural bristle brush to exfoliate the skin and stimulate lymphatic flow. Dry brushing before a shower can help remove dead skin cells and promote detoxification through the skin.

7. **Adequate Sleep**: Restful sleep is crucial for detoxification, as the body performs many detox processes during sleep. Creating a sleep-friendly environment and maintaining a regular sleep schedule support overall health and effective detoxification.

8. **Stress Management**: Chronic stress can impede detoxification processes. Incorporating stress-reducing practices like meditation, deep breathing exercises, and spending time in nature can support the body's detox functions. The mind-body connection plays a significant role in overall health, making mental well-being essential for effective detoxification.

Safety and Precautions

While detoxification can offer significant health benefits, it's essential to approach it safely. Here are some safety tips:

- **Consult a Healthcare Professional**: Especially if you have underlying health conditions or are taking medications, consult with a healthcare provider before starting any detox program.

- **Start Slowly**: Gradually introduce detox practices to avoid overwhelming your system.

- **Stay Hydrated**: Ensure adequate hydration throughout any detox program.

- **Monitor Your Body**: Pay attention to how your body responds and adjust accordingly. If you experience severe symptoms, stop the detox and seek medical advice.

Detoxification is a vital aspect of maintaining optimal health and well-being. By understanding the importance of detoxifying the body and incorporating practical, safe, and effective strategies, you can support your body's natural ability to cleanse and heal. This chapter provides a comprehensive guide to integrating detox practices into your daily life, empowering you to take control of your health and experience the benefits of a cleaner, more vibrant body.

Detox Foods

1. **Leafy Greens**
   - **Kale, Spinach, and Swiss Chard**: Rich in chlorophyll, these greens help detoxify the liver and support overall digestion. Incorporating a variety of leafy greens into your diet is essential for their numerous health benefits.

2. **Cruciferous Vegetables**
   - **Broccoli, Cauliflower, and Brussels Sprouts**: These vegetables contain compounds that support liver detoxification processes. Regular consumption can help the body neutralize and eliminate toxins more effectively.

3. **Berries**
   - **Blueberries, Raspberries, and Strawberries**: Packed with antioxidants, berries help combat oxidative stress and inflammation, two key factors in detoxification. Barbara recommends including a handful of berries in the diet daily to enhance overall health.

4. **Citrus Fruits**

    o **Lemons, Oranges, and Grapefruits**: High in vitamin C and other antioxidants, citrus fruits support the body's detoxification enzymes. Starting the day with a glass of warm lemon water is a simple yet effective detox strategy.

5. **Herbs and Spices**

    o **Turmeric, Ginger, and Garlic**: These potent anti-inflammatory and antioxidant herbs and spices aid in detoxification and boost the immune system.

6. **Green Tea**

    o **Rich in Catechins**: Green tea contains catechins, which enhance liver function and promote the elimination of toxins. Drinking several cups of green tea daily can support detoxification and overall wellness.

7. **Probiotic-Rich Foods**

    o **Yogurt, Sauerkraut, and Kimchi**: These foods support gut health by maintaining a healthy balance of gut bacteria, which is crucial for effective detoxification.

8. **Nuts and Seeds**

    o **Flaxseeds, Chia Seeds, and Almonds**: These are excellent sources of fiber, healthy fats, and other nutrients that support detoxification. Including a variety of nuts and seeds in the diet can help maintain regular bowel movements and support overall health.

Incorporating natural detox methods and foods into your daily routine can significantly enhance your body's ability to eliminate toxins and promote overall health. By following these guidelines, you can achieve a balanced and healthy state, allowing your body to function at its best.

Chapter 4: Boosting Immunity Naturally

Boosting your immune system naturally is a crucial aspect of maintaining overall health and well-being. A strong immune system helps protect against infections, reduces the severity of illnesses, and promotes faster recovery. This chapter explores various herbs and foods that can enhance immune support.

Herbs and Foods for Immune Support

1. Echinacea (Echinacea purpurea)

Key Elements: Echinacea is renowned for its immune-boosting properties. It stimulates the production of white blood cells and enhances the body's ability to fight infections.

- **Active Compounds**: Polysaccharides, flavonoids, and alkamides.

- **Uses Against Diseases**: Echinacea is commonly used to prevent and treat colds, flu, and other respiratory infections. It can also reduce the duration and severity of symptoms.

- **Preparation Methods**: Echinacea can be consumed as a tea, tincture, or capsule. For tea, steep 1-2 teaspoons of dried echinacea in hot water for 10-15 minutes. Tinctures can be taken as 2-3 ml up to three times daily.

- **Dosage, Safety, and Precautions**: Recommended dose is 300 mg of echinacea extract three times daily. It is generally safe for short-term use but may cause mild side effects like stomach upset. People with autoimmune disorders should consult a healthcare provider before use.

2. Garlic (Allium sativum)

Key Elements: Garlic is a potent immune booster with antibacterial, antiviral, and antifungal properties. It enhances the immune response and helps the body ward off infections.

- **Active Compounds**: Allicin, sulfur compounds.

- **Uses Against Diseases**: Garlic is effective against colds, flu, and other infections. It also supports cardiovascular health by lowering blood pressure and cholesterol levels.

- **Preparation Methods**: Garlic can be eaten raw, cooked, or taken as a supplement. Crushing or chopping garlic and letting it sit for 10 minutes before use can maximize allicin production.

- **Dosage, Safety, and Precautions**: Consume 1-2 cloves of raw garlic daily or 600-1200 mg of aged garlic extract. Garlic is generally safe but may cause bad breath, body odor, or gastrointestinal discomfort in some people.

3. Ginger (Zingiber officinale)

Key Elements: Ginger has anti-inflammatory and antioxidant properties, making it an excellent herb for boosting immunity. It helps reduce inflammation and oxidative stress in the body.

- **Active Compounds**: Gingerol, shogaol, and zingerone.

- **Uses Against Diseases**: Ginger is effective in treating respiratory infections, sore throats, and inflammation. It also aids digestion and alleviates nausea.

- **Preparation Methods**: Ginger can be consumed as a tea, added to foods, or taken as a supplement. For tea, steep 1-2 teaspoons of fresh grated ginger in hot water for 10-15 minutes.

- **Dosage, Safety, and Precautions**: Recommended dose is 1-3 grams of ginger daily. Ginger is generally safe but may cause heartburn or stomach upset in some individuals.

4. Elderberry (Sambucus nigra)

Key Elements: Elderberry is rich in antioxidants and vitamins that support immune health. It has been traditionally used to prevent and treat colds and flu.

- **Active Compounds**: Anthocyanins, flavonoids, and vitamin C.

- **Uses Against Diseases**: Elderberry is effective against colds, flu, and sinus infections. It can reduce the duration and severity of symptoms.

- **Preparation Methods**: Elderberry can be consumed as a syrup, tea, or supplement. To make elderberry syrup, simmer 1 cup of dried elderberries with 4 cups of water until reduced by half, then strain and add honey.

- **Dosage, Safety, and Precautions**: Take 1-2 tablespoons of elderberry syrup daily. Raw elderberries are toxic and should not be consumed without proper preparation. Consult a healthcare provider before use, especially during pregnancy or if you have an autoimmune condition.

5. Turmeric (Curcuma longa)

Key Elements: Turmeric is known for its powerful anti-inflammatory and antioxidant properties. It supports the immune system by reducing inflammation and oxidative stress.

- **Active Compounds**: Curcumin, volatile oils.

- **Uses Against Diseases**: Turmeric is effective in managing inflammatory conditions, boosting immune function, and supporting overall health.

- **Preparation Methods**: Turmeric can be added to foods, taken as a tea, or used as a supplement. For tea, simmer 1 teaspoon of turmeric powder in water for 10 minutes, then strain.

- **Dosage, Safety, and Precautions**: Recommended dose is 500-2000 mg of turmeric extract daily. Turmeric is generally safe but may cause digestive issues in high doses. People with gallbladder disease should avoid turmeric supplements.

6. Astragalus (Astragalus membranaceus)

Key Elements: Astragalus is an adaptogenic herb that enhances the body's resistance to stress and boosts the immune system. It is particularly effective in preventing colds and respiratory infections.

- **Active Compounds**: Polysaccharides, saponins, flavonoids.

- **Uses Against Diseases**: Astragalus is used to prevent colds, flu, and respiratory infections. It also supports overall vitality and longevity.

- **Preparation Methods**: Astragalus can be taken as a tea, tincture, or supplement. For tea, simmer 1-2 teaspoons of dried astragalus root in water for 20-30 minutes.

- **Dosage, Safety, and Precautions**: Recommended dose is 250-500 mg of astragalus extract up to three times daily. Astragalus is generally safe but may interact with immune-suppressing medications.

7. Reishi Mushroom (Ganoderma lucidum)

Key Elements: Reishi mushroom is a powerful immune booster and adaptogen. It supports immune function and helps the body adapt to stress.

- **Active Compounds**: Polysaccharides, triterpenes, peptidoglycans.

- **Uses Against Diseases**: Reishi mushroom is effective in preventing and treating infections, reducing inflammation, and enhancing overall vitality.

- **Preparation Methods**: Reishi can be taken as a tea, tincture, or supplement. For tea, simmer 1-2 slices of dried reishi mushroom in water for 30-45 minutes.

- **Dosage, Safety, and Precautions**: Recommended dose is 1-2 grams of reishi extract daily. Reishi is generally safe but may cause mild digestive issues in some individuals.

8. Green Tea (Camellia sinensis)

Key Elements: Green tea is rich in antioxidants and polyphenols that support immune health. It helps reduce oxidative stress and inflammation in the body.

- **Active Compounds**: Catechins, epigallocatechin gallate (EGCG).

- **Uses Against Diseases**: Green tea is effective in boosting immune function, reducing the risk of infections, and supporting overall health.

- **Preparation Methods**: Green tea can be brewed as a tea or taken as a supplement. For tea, steep 1-2 teaspoons of green tea leaves in hot water for 2-3 minutes.

- **Dosage, Safety, and Precautions**: Recommended dose is 2-3 cups of green tea daily or 300-400 mg of green tea extract. Green tea is generally safe but may cause insomnia or stomach upset in some individuals.

9. Vitamin C-Rich Foods

Key Elements: Vitamin C is a crucial nutrient for immune health. It supports the production and function of white blood cells, which help fight infections.

- **Active Compounds**: Ascorbic acid.

- **Uses Against Diseases**: Vitamin C-rich foods help prevent and treat colds, flu, and other infections. They also support overall health and well-being.

- **Preparation Methods**: Consume foods rich in vitamin C, such as citrus fruits, bell peppers, strawberries, kiwi, and broccoli. These can be eaten raw, juiced, or included in meals.

- **Dosage, Safety, and Precautions**: Aim for 75-90 mg of vitamin C daily from food sources. High doses of vitamin C supplements can cause digestive issues.

10. Probiotic Foods

Key Elements: Probiotics are beneficial bacteria that support gut health and immune function. A healthy gut microbiome is essential for a robust immune system.

- **Active Compounds**: Live beneficial bacteria such as Lactobacillus and Bifidobacterium.

- **Uses Against Diseases**: Probiotic foods help prevent and treat infections, support digestion, and enhance overall immune health.

- **Preparation Methods**: Consume probiotic-rich foods such as yogurt, kefir, sauerkraut, kimchi, and kombucha. These can be included in daily meals.

- **Dosage, Safety, and Precautions**: Incorporate a variety of probiotic foods into your diet. Probiotics are generally safe but may cause mild digestive issues in some individuals.

Incorporating these herbs and foods into your daily routine can significantly boost your immune system naturally. These natural remedies emphasize the importance of supporting the body's innate ability to heal and protect itself. By making informed choices about what you consume, you can enhance your immune function and overall health, leading to a more resilient and vibrant life.

Lifestyle Changes for a Resilient Immune System

Creating a resilient immune system requires more than just temporary measures; it involves adopting sustainable lifestyle changes that support your overall health and well-being. Here are comprehensive lifestyle changes that can help fortify your immune system and promote long-term health.

1. Balanced Nutrition

Importance: Nutrition is the cornerstone of a robust immune system. A balanced diet provides the essential nutrients needed for the body to function optimally and fend off illnesses.

Key Practices:

- **Whole Foods**: Focus on whole, unprocessed foods rich in vitamins, minerals, and antioxidants. These include fruits, vegetables, whole grains, nuts, seeds, and lean proteins.

- **Superfoods**: Incorporate immune-boosting superfoods such as garlic, ginger, turmeric, and green leafy vegetables into your diet.

- **Healthy Fats**: Include sources of healthy fats like avocados, nuts, seeds, and olive oil to support cellular health and reduce inflammation.

- **Reduce Sugar and Processed Foods**: Minimize intake of sugar and processed foods, which can suppress immune function and promote inflammation.

2. Regular Physical Activity

Importance: Regular exercise enhances immune function by improving circulation, reducing stress, and promoting the efficient movement of immune cells throughout the body.

Key Practices:

- **Consistency**: Aim for at least 150 minutes of moderate aerobic activity or 75 minutes of vigorous activity per week, combined with muscle-strengthening exercises.

- **Variety**: Incorporate a mix of cardiovascular exercises, strength training, flexibility exercises, and activities that promote balance.

- **Enjoyable Activities**: Engage in physical activities that you enjoy, such as walking, swimming, dancing, or yoga, to ensure long-term adherence.

3. Quality Sleep

Importance: Adequate sleep is vital for immune health, allowing the body to repair, regenerate, and produce critical immune cells and proteins.

Key Practices:

- **Sleep Hygiene**: Maintain a regular sleep schedule, creating a bedtime routine that promotes relaxation, such as reading, meditation, or a warm bath.

- **Sleep Environment**: Ensure your sleep environment is conducive to rest—dark, quiet, and cool. Use blackout curtains, earplugs, or white noise machines if necessary.

- **Limit Stimulants**: Avoid caffeine, heavy meals, and electronic screens close to bedtime.

4. Stress Management

Importance: Chronic stress can weaken the immune system, making the body more susceptible to infections and diseases.

Key Practices:

- **Mindfulness and Meditation**: Practice mindfulness and meditation to reduce stress and improve emotional resilience.

- **Deep Breathing Exercises**: Engage in deep breathing exercises to activate the parasympathetic nervous system and promote relaxation.

- **Prayer and Reflection**: Incorporate prayer or reflective practices into your daily routine to foster a sense of peace and connection.

- **Time Management**: Develop effective time management strategies to balance work, rest, and leisure, preventing burnout and reducing stress.

5. Hydration

Importance: Staying hydrated is essential for maintaining the health of every cell in the body, including those of the immune system.

Key Practices:

- **Water Intake**: Drink plenty of water throughout the day. Aim for at least eight 8-ounce glasses, or more if you are physically active or live in a hot climate.

- **Hydrating Foods**: Consume hydrating foods such as cucumbers, watermelon, oranges, and strawberries.

- **Limit Dehydrating Beverages**: Reduce consumption of caffeinated and alcoholic beverages, which can lead to dehydration.

6. Social Connections

Importance: Strong social connections and a supportive community can enhance mental health and boost immune function.

Key Practices:

- **Stay Connected**: Maintain regular contact with friends and family through calls, video chats, or in-person visits.

- **Community Involvement**: Participate in community activities, clubs, or support groups that interest you.

- **Acts of Kindness**: Engage in acts of kindness and volunteer work, which can boost your mood and overall well-being.

7. Exposure to Nature

Importance: Spending time in nature can reduce stress, enhance mood, and improve overall health.

Key Practices:

- **Regular Outdoor Activities**: Incorporate outdoor activities such as hiking, gardening, or simply walking in the park into your routine.

- **Sunlight Exposure**: Aim for at least 15-30 minutes of sunlight exposure daily to boost vitamin D levels, essential for immune health.

8. Personal Hygiene

Importance: Good hygiene practices can prevent infections and support overall immune health.

Key Practices:

- **Hand Washing**: Wash your hands regularly with soap and water, especially before eating and after being in public places.

- **Oral Hygiene**: Maintain good oral hygiene by brushing and flossing daily to prevent infections.

- **Clean Environment**: Keep your living space clean and sanitized to reduce exposure to pathogens.

9. Herbal Support

Importance: Certain herbs and supplements can provide additional immune support, enhancing the body's natural defenses.

Key Practices:

- **Herbal Teas and Tinctures**: Incorporate immune-boosting herbs such as echinacea, elderberry, and astragalus into your daily routine through teas and tinctures.

- **Dietary Supplements**: Consider supplements like vitamin C, vitamin D, zinc, and probiotics, especially during flu season or times of increased stress.

- **Consistent Use**: Regularly use these herbs and supplements for continuous immune support, as advised by Barbara O'Neill.

By integrating these lifestyle changes into your daily routine, you can create a resilient immune system that is well-equipped to defend against illness and promote long-term health. These practices, emphasize the importance of nurturing the body, mind, and spirit to achieve optimal wellness. Consistency and commitment to these habits will not only enhance your immune function but also improve your overall quality of life.

Chapter 5: Digestive Health and Herbal Remedies

Digestive health is a cornerstone of overall well-being, and understanding common digestive issues along with their symptoms is essential for maintaining optimal gut health. Digestive problems can range from mild discomfort to severe conditions that significantly impact quality of life. Here, we will explore some of the most prevalent digestive issues, their symptoms, and how they can be identified and managed.

The Importance of a Proper Acid-Alkaline Balance

The concept of acid-alkaline balance is crucial for optimal health. The pH level, which measures acidity and alkalinity, significantly influences bodily functions, impacting everything from digestion to immunity. This chapter explores the importance of maintaining a proper acid-alkaline balance and provides practical insights on how to achieve and sustain it.

Understanding pH Balance

The pH scale ranges from 0 to 14, with 7 being neutral. A pH below 7 indicates acidity, while a pH above 7 indicates alkalinity. The human body functions best when its internal environment is slightly alkaline, typically around a pH of 7.4.

Why pH Balance Matters

1. **Enzyme Function**: Enzymes, which drive nearly all biochemical reactions in the body, require a specific pH range to function optimally.

2. **Metabolic Processes**: Proper pH balance is essential for efficient metabolic processes, including energy production and nutrient absorption.

3. **Immune System**: An alkaline environment supports immune function, helping to ward off infections and diseases.

4. **Bone Health**: Maintaining a slightly alkaline pH helps prevent the body from leaching calcium from bones to neutralize excess acidity, thus protecting against osteoporosis.

Consequences of Imbalance

An imbalanced pH can lead to various health issues:

- **Acidosis**: Excess acidity can cause fatigue, headaches, confusion, and increased risk of chronic diseases like diabetes and cancer.

- **Alkalosis**: Excess alkalinity, though less common, can lead to muscle twitching, nausea, and confusion.

Factors Affecting pH Balance

Several factors influence the body's pH, including diet, lifestyle, and stress levels. Processed foods, sugars, and high-stress levels contribute to acidity, while a diet rich in vegetables, fruits, and proper hydration promotes alkalinity.

Practical Insights on Maintaining Acid-Alkaline Balance

1. **Dietary Changes**:

    o **Increase Alkaline-Forming Foods**: Incorporate more vegetables (especially leafy greens), fruits, nuts, and seeds into your diet.

    o **Reduce Acid-Forming Foods**: Limit intake of processed foods, sugars, red meats, and dairy products.

    o **Balanced Meals**: Aim for a balanced plate with a higher proportion of alkaline-forming foods to neutralize acidic effects.

2. **Hydration**:

    o **Water Intake**: Drink plenty of water throughout the day to help flush out toxins and maintain pH balance.

    o **Alkaline Water**: Consider drinking alkaline water, which can help balance your body's pH levels.

3. **Natural Supplements**:

    o **Lemon Water**: Start your day with a glass of lemon water. Despite being acidic, lemon has an alkalizing effect on the body.

    o **Apple Cider Vinegar**: Consuming apple cider vinegar diluted in water can aid digestion and support pH balance.

4. **Lifestyle Adjustments**:

    o **Exercise**: Regular physical activity helps maintain pH balance by promoting efficient metabolic processes.

    o **Stress Management**: Practices like meditation, yoga, and deep breathing can reduce stress, which in turn helps maintain pH balance.

5. **Regular Monitoring**:

    o **pH Testing**: Use pH strips to regularly test your saliva or urine pH levels. This can provide insights into how your diet and lifestyle are affecting your acid-alkaline balance.

Maintaining a proper acid-alkaline balance is fundamental for overall health and well-being. By making mindful dietary choices, staying hydrated, incorporating natural supplements, and adopting healthy lifestyle practices, you can achieve and sustain an optimal pH balance. This holistic approach not only enhances physical health but also supports mental and emotional well-being, paving the way for a healthier, more balanced life.

Gastroesophageal Reflux Disease (GERD)

Overview: GERD is a chronic condition where stomach acid flows back into the esophagus, causing irritation and discomfort. It occurs when the lower esophageal sphincter (LES) fails to close properly, allowing acid to escape from the stomach.

Symptoms:

- Heartburn: A burning sensation in the chest, often after eating, which might be worse at night.

- Regurgitation: Sour or bitter-tasting acid backing up into the throat or mouth.

- Dysphagia: Difficulty swallowing.

- Chest pain.

- Chronic cough or throat irritation.

- Hoarseness or a sore throat.

Peppermint Tea

- **Ingredients**: Fresh or dried peppermint leaves (1-2 teaspoons), 1 cup of boiling water.
- **Instructions**:
    1. Place the peppermint leaves in a teapot or cup.
    2. Pour boiling water over the leaves.
    3. Cover and let steep for 10 minutes.
    4. Strain the tea and drink warm.
    o **Dosage**: Drink 1-2 cups daily, especially after meals.
    o **Precautions**: Avoid if you have a hiatal hernia or severe GERD as it may worsen symptoms in some individuals.

Chamomile Tea

- **Ingredients**: 2-3 teaspoons of dried chamomile flowers, 1 cup of boiling water.
- **Instructions**:
    1. Place chamomile flowers in a teapot or cup.
    2. Pour boiling water over the flowers.
    3. Cover and steep for 5-10 minutes.
    4. Strain and drink warm.
    - **Dosage**: Drink 2-3 cups daily.
    - **Precautions**: Avoid if allergic to ragweed, daisies, marigolds, or chrysanthemums.

Slippery Elm Lozenges

- **Ingredients**: Slippery elm powder (1 teaspoon), a small amount of water or honey.
- **Instructions**:
    1. Mix the slippery elm powder with enough water or honey to form a thick paste.
    2. Shape into small lozenges and let dry.
    3. Suck on a lozenge as needed for relief.
    - **Dosage**: Use 2-4 lozenges daily.
    - **Precautions**: Generally safe, but drink plenty of water to prevent choking.

Constipation

Overview: Constipation is characterized by infrequent bowel movements or difficulty passing stools. It can be caused by a variety of factors, including a lack of fiber in the diet, dehydration, lack of physical activity, and certain medications.

Symptoms:

- Fewer than three bowel movements per week.
- Hard, dry, or lumpy stools.
- Straining during bowel movements.

- A feeling of blockage in the rectum.

- The sensation of incomplete evacuation.

Flaxseed Water

- **Ingredients**: 1 tablespoon whole flaxseeds, 1 cup of water.

- **Instructions**:

    1. Add the flaxseeds to the water and let soak overnight.

    2. Stir and drink the water (including the seeds) in the morning.

    o **Dosage**: Drink 1 cup daily.

    o **Precautions**: Drink plenty of water throughout the day to prevent blockage.

Dandelion Root Tea

- **Ingredients**: 1-2 teaspoons dried dandelion root, 1 cup of boiling water.

- **Instructions**:

    1. Place dandelion root in a teapot or cup.

    2. Pour boiling water over the root.

    3. Cover and steep for 10-15 minutes.

    4. Strain and drink warm.

    o **Dosage**: Drink 2-3 cups daily.

    o **Precautions**: Avoid if allergic to dandelion or related plants.

Senna Tea

- **Ingredients**: 1-2 grams of dried senna leaves, 1 cup of boiling water.

- **Instructions**:

    1. Place senna leaves in a teapot or cup.

    2. Pour boiling water over the leaves.

    3. Cover and steep for 5-10 minutes.

4. Strain and drink warm.

- o **Dosage**: Drink 1 cup before bedtime.

- o **Precautions**: Do not use for more than 7 consecutive days to avoid dependency.

Diarrhea

Overview: Diarrhea is characterized by loose, watery stools and an increased frequency of bowel movements. It can be caused by infections, food intolerances, medications, and other underlying health conditions.

Symptoms:

- Frequent, loose, or watery stools.

- Abdominal cramps and pain.

- Urgency to have a bowel movement.

- Nausea or vomiting.

- Dehydration symptoms, such as dry mouth, dizziness, or reduced urine output.

Chamomile and Peppermint Tea

- **Ingredients**: 1 teaspoon dried chamomile flowers, 1 teaspoon dried peppermint leaves, 1 cup boiling water.

- **Instructions**:

  1. Combine chamomile flowers and peppermint leaves in a teapot or cup.

  2. Pour boiling water over the mixture.

  3. Cover and steep for 10 minutes.

  4. Strain and drink warm.

  - o **Dosage**: Drink 2-3 cups daily.

  - o **Precautions**: Avoid if allergic to any of the ingredients.

Slippery Elm Gruel

- **Ingredients**: 1 tablespoon slippery elm powder, 1 cup warm water or milk.
- **Instructions**:

    1. Mix slippery elm powder with warm water or milk to form a smooth paste.

    2. Consume immediately.

    o **Dosage**: Consume 1-2 times daily.

    o **Precautions**: Drink plenty of water to avoid choking.

Blackberry Leaf Tea

- **Ingredients**: 1-2 teaspoons dried blackberry leaves, 1 cup boiling water.
- **Instructions**:

    1. Place blackberry leaves in a teapot or cup.

    2. Pour boiling water over the leaves.

    3. Cover and steep for 10 minutes.

    4. Strain and drink warm.

    o **Dosage**: Drink 2-3 cups daily.

    o **Precautions**: Generally safe, but avoid if pregnant or breastfeeding without medical advice.

Peptic Ulcers

Overview: Peptic ulcers are sores that develop on the lining of the stomach, small intestine, or esophagus. They are often caused by an infection with Helicobacter pylori bacteria or prolonged use of nonsteroidal anti-inflammatory drugs (NSAIDs).

Symptoms:

- Burning stomach pain.
- Bloating and belching.
- Fatty food intolerance.
- Heartburn.
- Nausea.

- In severe cases, vomiting blood or having black, tarry stools.

Licorice Root Tea

- **Ingredients**: 1 teaspoon dried licorice root, 1 cup boiling water.
- **Instructions**:
    1. Place licorice root in a teapot or cup.
    2. Pour boiling water over the root.
    3. Cover and steep for 10-15 minutes.
    4. Strain and drink warm.
    o **Dosage**: Drink 2-3 cups daily.
    o **Precautions**: Use deglycyrrhizinated licorice (DGL) to avoid side effects.

Marshmallow Root Tea

- **Ingredients**: 1-2 teaspoons dried marshmallow root, 1 cup cold water.
- **Instructions**:
    1. Place marshmallow root in a teapot or cup.
    2. Pour cold water over the root and let steep overnight.
    3. Strain and drink cold.
    o **Dosage**: Drink 2-3 cups daily.
    o **Precautions**: Generally safe, but drink plenty of water.

Inflammatory Bowel Disease (IBD)

Overview: IBD is an umbrella term for chronic inflammatory conditions of the gastrointestinal tract, primarily including Crohn's disease and ulcerative colitis. The exact cause is unknown, but it involves an abnormal immune response.

Symptoms:

- Persistent diarrhea.

- Abdominal pain and cramping.

- Blood in the stool.

- Reduced appetite and weight loss.

- Fatigue.

- Fever.

Aloe Vera Juice

- **Ingredients**: Fresh aloe vera gel (2 tablespoons), 1 cup of water or juice.
- **Instructions**:
    1. Blend the aloe vera gel with water or juice.
    2. Drink immediately.
    o **Dosage**: Drink 1/2 cup 2-3 times daily.
    o **Precautions**: Ensure the aloe vera is properly prepared to avoid potential side effects.

Turmeric and Ginger Tea

- **Ingredients**: 1 teaspoon turmeric powder, 1-inch piece of fresh ginger, 2 cups of water.
- **Instructions**:
    1. Peel and slice the ginger.
    2. Boil the ginger slices and turmeric powder in water for 10 minutes.
    3. Strain and drink warm.
    o **Dosage**: Drink 1-2 cups daily.
    o **Precautions**: Consult with a healthcare provider if you have gallbladder issues.

Boswellia Supplement

- **Ingredients**: Boswellia serrata extract capsules.
- **Instructions**:
    1. Purchase Boswellia serrata extract capsules from a reputable supplier.

2. Follow the dosage instructions provided on the packaging.

o **Dosage**: Typically 300-500 mg, 2-3 times daily.

o **Precautions**: Generally safe, but consult with a healthcare provider if pregnant or breastfeeding.

Celiac Disease

Overview: Celiac disease is an autoimmune disorder where ingestion of gluten leads to damage in the small intestine. It affects nutrient absorption and can lead to various complications if left untreated.

Symptoms:

- Diarrhea or constipation.
- Bloating and gas.
- Abdominal pain.
- Fatigue.
- Anemia.
- Weight loss.
- Skin rash (dermatitis herpetiformis).

Marshmallow Root Tea

- **Ingredients**: 1-2 teaspoons dried marshmallow root, 1 cup cold water.
- **Instructions**:
    1. Place marshmallow root in a teapot or cup.
    2. Pour cold water over the root and let steep overnight.
    3. Strain and drink cold.
    o **Dosage**: Drink 2-3 cups daily.
    o **Precautions**: Generally safe, but drink plenty of water.

Slippery Elm Gruel

- **Ingredients**: 1 tablespoon slippery elm powder, 1 cup warm water or milk.
- **Instructions**:

    1. Mix slippery elm powder with warm water or milk to form a smooth paste.

    2. Consume immediately.

    o **Dosage**: Consume 1-2 times daily.

    o **Precautions**: Drink plenty of water to avoid choking.

Gallstones

Overview: Gallstones are hardened deposits of digestive fluid that can form in the gallbladder. They can block the bile ducts and cause pain, infection, or inflammation.

Symptoms:

- Sudden and intense pain in the upper right abdomen.

- Pain between the shoulder blades.

- Nausea or vomiting.

- Indigestion or gas.

- Jaundice (yellowing of the skin and eyes) if the bile duct is blocked.

Dandelion Root Tea

- **Ingredients**: 1-2 teaspoons dried dandelion root, 1 cup of boiling water.
- **Instructions**:

    1. Place dandelion root in a teapot or cup.

    2. Pour boiling water over the root.

    3. Cover and steep for 10-15 minutes.

    4. Strain and drink warm.

    o **Dosage**: Drink 2-3 cups daily.

    o **Precautions**: Avoid if allergic to dandelion or related plants.

Milk Thistle Tea

- **Ingredients**: 1-2 teaspoons crushed milk thistle seeds, 1 cup boiling water.
- **Instructions**:

  1. Place milk thistle seeds in a teapot or cup.
  2. Pour boiling water over the seeds.
  3. Cover and steep for 10-15 minutes.
  4. Strain and drink warm.
  - **Dosage**: Drink 2-3 cups daily.
  - **Precautions**: Generally safe, but consult with a healthcare provider if pregnant or breastfeeding.

Peppermint Oil Capsules

- **Ingredients**: Enteric-coated peppermint oil capsules.
- **Instructions**:

  1. Purchase enteric-coated peppermint oil capsules from a reputable supplier.
  2. Follow the dosage instructions provided on the packaging.
  - **Dosage**: Typically 1-2 capsules, 2-3 times daily before meals.
  - **Precautions**: Ensure capsules are enteric-coated to avoid heartburn.

Lactose Intolerance

Overview: Lactose intolerance occurs when the body cannot digest lactose, a sugar found in milk and dairy products, due to a deficiency in the enzyme lactase.

Symptoms:

- Diarrhea.
- Bloating.
- Gas.

- Abdominal cramps.

- Nausea.

Ginger Tea

- **Ingredients**: Fresh ginger root (1-2 inches), 2 cups of water.

- **Instructions**:

  1. Peel and slice the ginger root.

  2. Boil the ginger slices in water for 10 minutes.

  3. Strain and drink warm.

  o **Dosage**: Drink 1-2 cups daily.

  o **Precautions**: Avoid excessive consumption if you have gallstones.

Chamomile Tea

- **Ingredients**: 2-3 teaspoons of dried chamomile flowers, 1 cup of boiling water.

- **Instructions**:

  1. Place chamomile flowers in a teapot or cup.

  2. Pour boiling water over the flowers.

  3. Cover and steep for 5-10 minutes.

  4. Strain and drink warm.

  o **Dosage**: Drink 2-3 cups daily.

  o **Precautions**: Avoid if allergic to ragweed, daisies, marigolds, or chrysanthemums.

Diverticulitis

Overview: Diverticulitis is the inflammation or infection of small pouches (diverticula) that can form in the walls of the digestive tract, often in the colon.

Symptoms:

- Severe abdominal pain, typically on the left side.

- Fever.

- Nausea and vomiting.

- Constipation or diarrhea.

- Bloating.

Slippery Elm Gruel

- **Ingredients**: 1 tablespoon slippery elm powder, 1 cup warm water or milk.

- **Instructions**:

    1. Mix slippery elm powder with warm water or milk to form a smooth paste.

    2. Consume immediately.

    o **Dosage**: Consume 1-2 times daily.

    o **Precautions**: Drink plenty of water to avoid choking.

Marshmallow Root Tea

- **Ingredients**: 1-2 teaspoons dried marshmallow root, 1 cup cold water.

- **Instructions**:

    1. Place marshmallow root in a teapot or cup.

    2. Pour cold water over the root and let steep overnight.

    3. Strain and drink cold.

    o **Dosage**: Drink 2-3 cups daily.

    o **Precautions**: Generally safe, but drink plenty of water.

Peppermint Tea

- **Ingredients**: Fresh or dried peppermint leaves (1-2 teaspoons), 1 cup of boiling water.

- **Instructions**:

    1. Place the peppermint leaves in a teapot or cup.

2. Pour boiling water over the leaves.

3. Cover and let steep for 10 minutes.

4. Strain the tea and drink warm.

o **Dosage**: Drink 1-2 cups daily, especially after meals.

o **Precautions**: Avoid if you have a hiatal hernia or severe GERD as it may worsen symptoms in some individuals.

Digestive health is vital for overall well-being, and understanding common digestive issues and their symptoms is the first step toward maintaining a healthy gut. By incorporating herbal and dietary interventions, along with lifestyle changes, you can support your digestive system and improve your quality of life.

Lifestyle Tips for Optimal Gut Health - Chronic Fatigue and IBS

Gut health is fundamental to overall well-being. The gastrointestinal tract, often referred to as the "second brain," plays a critical role in nutrient absorption, immune function, and even mental health. In this chapter, we'll explore the intricate relationship between gut health, chronic fatigue, and Irritable Bowel Syndrome (IBS), providing practical advice on managing these conditions through diet, natural remedies, and lifestyle changes.

The Importance of Gut Health

The gut is home to trillions of bacteria that form the microbiome. This complex ecosystem is crucial for digesting food, absorbing nutrients, and protecting against pathogens. When the microbiome is out of balance, it can lead to various health issues, including chronic fatigue and IBS.

- **Microbiome Balance**: A healthy gut microbiome supports efficient digestion and strong immunity. Probiotics (beneficial bacteria) and prebiotics (food for these bacteria) are essential for maintaining this balance.

- **Gut-Brain Connection**: The gut communicates with the brain through the vagus nerve, influencing mood and stress levels. An imbalance in the gut can contribute to mental health issues and chronic fatigue.

Chronic Fatigue and Gut Health

Chronic fatigue syndrome (CFS) is characterized by extreme tiredness that doesn't improve with rest. Gut health plays a significant role in this condition.

- **Nutrient Absorption**: Poor gut health can lead to nutrient deficiencies, which can cause fatigue. Ensuring adequate intake of vitamins and minerals through a balanced diet can help.

- **Inflammation**: Chronic inflammation in the gut can spread throughout the body, leading to systemic fatigue. Anti-inflammatory foods and supplements can reduce this inflammation.

Natural Remedies

Incorporating natural remedies can support gut health and manage symptoms of chronic fatigue and IBS.

- **Probiotics**: Consuming probiotic-rich foods like yogurt, kefir, sauerkraut, and kimchi can help maintain a healthy microbiome.

- **Herbal Remedies**: Herbs like ginger, peppermint, and aloe vera can soothe the digestive tract and reduce inflammation.

- **Detoxification**: Regular detoxification can help eliminate toxins that disrupt gut health. Methods include drinking lemon water, consuming detoxifying foods like leafy greens, and avoiding processed foods.

Lifestyle Adjustments

In addition to dietary changes, lifestyle adjustments are crucial for maintaining gut health and managing chronic fatigue and IBS.

- **Stress Management**: Stress can negatively impact gut health. Techniques like meditation, yoga, and deep breathing exercises can help manage stress levels.

- **Regular Exercise**: Physical activity promotes healthy digestion and reduces stress. Aim for at least 30 minutes of moderate exercise most days of the week.

- **Adequate Sleep**: Quality sleep is essential for gut health and overall well-being. Establish a regular sleep routine and ensure you get 7-9 hours of sleep per night.

Maintaining gut health is vital for preventing and managing chronic fatigue and IBS. By adopting a holistic approach that includes a balanced diet, natural remedies, and healthy lifestyle practices, you can improve your gut health and overall quality of life. This chapter has provided practical advice and insights into the intricate relationship between the gut, chronic fatigue, and IBS, empowering you to take control of your health naturally.

1. Balanced Diet Rich in Fiber

A diet high in fiber is essential for a healthy gut. Fiber promotes regular bowel movements, prevents constipation, and feeds beneficial gut bacteria.

- **Whole Grains**: Incorporate whole grains like brown rice, quinoa, oats, and barley into your diet. These grains are rich in fiber and provide essential nutrients.

- **Fruits and Vegetables**: Consume a variety of colorful fruits and vegetables daily. They are packed with fiber, vitamins, and minerals. Examples include berries, apples, pears, carrots, broccoli, and leafy greens.

- **Legumes**: Beans, lentils, and chickpeas are excellent sources of fiber and plant-based protein.

2. Stay Hydrated

Proper hydration is vital for digestive health. Water helps break down food, absorb nutrients, and eliminate waste.

- **Daily Water Intake**: Aim for at least 8 glasses of water per day. This can vary based on individual needs, activity levels, and climate.

- **Hydrating Foods**: Include water-rich foods like cucumbers, watermelon, and oranges in your diet.

3. Regular Physical Activity

Exercise stimulates the digestive system, reducing the risk of constipation and promoting regular bowel movements.

- **Daily Exercise**: Engage in at least 30 minutes of moderate exercise daily, such as walking, swimming, cycling, or yoga.

- **Core Strengthening**: Incorporate exercises that strengthen your core muscles, as a strong core supports the digestive organs.

4. Probiotics and Fermented Foods

Probiotics are beneficial bacteria that support gut health. Fermented foods are rich in probiotics and can help balance the gut microbiome.

- **Yogurt and Kefir**: Choose plain, unsweetened varieties with live and active cultures.

- **Sauerkraut and Kimchi**: These fermented vegetables are rich in probiotics and fiber.

- **Miso and Tempeh**: Fermented soy products that provide beneficial bacteria and protein.

5. Adequate Sleep

Quality sleep is essential for overall health, including gut health. Poor sleep can disrupt the gut microbiome and contribute to digestive issues.

- **Sleep Hygiene**: Maintain a regular sleep schedule, create a calming bedtime routine, and ensure your sleep environment is conducive to rest.
- **Avoid Stimulants**: Limit caffeine and electronic device use before bedtime to improve sleep quality.

6. Stress Management

Chronic stress negatively impacts gut health, leading to issues such as IBS, acid reflux, and ulcers.

- **Relaxation Techniques**: Practice relaxation techniques like deep breathing, meditation, and progressive muscle relaxation.
- **Physical Activity**: Regular exercise, such as yoga and tai chi, can help manage stress levels.
- **Hobbies and Interests**: Engage in activities that bring you joy and relaxation, such as reading, gardening, or painting.

7. Mindful Eating

Eating mindfully can improve digestion and prevent overeating. It allows you to focus on the eating experience and recognize hunger and fullness cues.

- **Chew Thoroughly**: Chew each bite thoroughly to aid in the digestive process.
- **Eat Slowly**: Take your time to enjoy your meals, which can help prevent indigestion and bloating.
- **Avoid Distractions**: Eat without distractions like television or smartphones to focus on your meal.

8. Limit Processed Foods and Sugars

Processed foods and excessive sugar can harm the gut microbiome and contribute to digestive issues.

- **Whole Foods**: Opt for whole, unprocessed foods whenever possible.
- **Read Labels**: Check ingredient labels to avoid added sugars, artificial sweeteners, and preservatives.

- **Healthy Alternatives**: Replace sugary snacks with healthier options like fruits, nuts, and seeds.

9. Regular Meal Times

Maintaining regular meal times helps regulate your digestive system and prevent issues such as acid reflux and indigestion.

- **Consistent Schedule**: Eat meals at roughly the same times each day.

- **Small, Frequent Meals**: Consider smaller, more frequent meals if you experience digestive discomfort after large meals.

10. Avoid Smoking and Excessive Alcohol

Both smoking and excessive alcohol consumption can damage the digestive system and lead to various gastrointestinal issues.

- **Quit Smoking**: Seek support and resources to help you quit smoking.

- **Moderate Alcohol**: Limit alcohol consumption to moderate levels or avoid it altogether for optimal gut health.

Adopting these lifestyle tips can significantly improve your digestive health and overall well-being. By following a balanced diet, staying hydrated, exercising regularly, and managing stress, you can support your digestive system and enhance your quality of life.

Chapter 6: Heart Health

Cardiovascular Ailments and Herbal Remedies

Cardiovascular ailments can range from mild to severe, affecting the heart and blood vessels, leading to conditions such as hypertension, atherosclerosis, angina, and heart failure. Below, we explore common cardiovascular ailments and provide detailed herbal remedies to support heart health.

1. Hypertension (High Blood Pressure)

Hypertension is a condition where the blood pressure in the arteries is persistently elevated, which can lead to serious health problems if left untreated.

Herbal Remedy: Hawthorn Berry Tea

Ingredients:

- 1 tablespoon dried hawthorn berries
- 2 cups water
- Honey (optional)

Instructions:

1. **Prepare the Berries**: Rinse the dried hawthorn berries under cold water.
2. **Boil the Water**: Bring 2 cups of water to a boil.
3. **Add the Berries**: Add the dried berries to the boiling water.
4. **Simmer**: Reduce the heat and let the berries simmer for about 10 minutes.
5. **Strain and Serve**: Strain the tea into a cup and sweeten with honey if desired. Drink this tea twice a day.

Hawthorn berries are known for their ability to dilate blood vessels, which can lower blood pressure and improve blood flow.

2. Atherosclerosis

Atherosclerosis is a condition where the arteries become narrowed and hardened due to plaque buildup, which can lead to heart attacks and strokes.

Herbal Remedy: Garlic and Lemon Infusion

Ingredients:

- 4 cloves garlic, minced

- 1 lemon, sliced

- 1 liter water

Instructions:

1. **Prepare the Ingredients**: Mince the garlic cloves and slice the lemon.

2. **Boil the Water**: Bring 1 liter of water to a boil.

3. **Add Ingredients**: Add the minced garlic and lemon slices to the boiling water.

4. **Simmer**: Reduce the heat and let the mixture simmer for 20 minutes.

5. **Cool and Strain**: Allow the infusion to cool, then strain it into a glass bottle.

6. **Storage**: Store the infusion in the refrigerator.

7. **Usage**: Drink a small glass (about 50 ml) of the infusion daily before breakfast.

Garlic is renowned for its ability to reduce cholesterol levels and prevent plaque buildup in the arteries, while lemon adds antioxidant properties.

3. Angina

Angina is chest pain or discomfort caused by reduced blood flow to the heart muscle. It is often a symptom of coronary artery disease.

Herbal Remedy: Ginger and Turmeric Tea

Ingredients:

- 1-inch piece of fresh ginger, sliced
- 1 teaspoon turmeric powder
- 2 cups water
- Honey (optional)

Instructions:

1. **Prepare the Ingredients**: Slice the ginger and measure out the turmeric powder.
2. **Boil the Water**: Bring 2 cups of water to a boil.
3. **Add the Ingredients**: Add the sliced ginger and turmeric powder to the boiling water.
4. **Simmer**: Reduce the heat and let the mixture simmer for 10 minutes.
5. **Strain and Serve**: Strain the tea into a cup and sweeten with honey if desired. Drink this tea twice a day.

Ginger improves blood circulation and turmeric reduces inflammation, both of which can help alleviate the symptoms of angina.

4. Heart Failure

Heart failure is a chronic condition where the heart cannot pump blood efficiently, leading to fatigue, shortness of breath, and fluid retention.

Herbal Remedy: Dandelion Leaf Tea

Ingredients:

- 1 tablespoon dried dandelion leaves
- 2 cups water
- Lemon juice (optional)

Instructions:

1. **Prepare the Leaves**: Rinse the dried dandelion leaves under cold water.

2. **Boil the Water**: Bring 2 cups of water to a boil.

3. **Add the Leaves**: Add the dried leaves to the boiling water.

4. **Simmer**: Reduce the heat and let the leaves simmer for 10 minutes.

5. **Strain and Serve**: Strain the tea into a cup and add a splash of lemon juice if desired. Drink this tea once daily.

Dandelion leaves act as a natural diuretic, helping to reduce fluid buildup and improve heart function.

5. Arrhythmia

Arrhythmia refers to an irregular heartbeat, which can be too fast, too slow, or erratic. It can be caused by various factors, including heart disease, stress, and electrolyte imbalances.

Herbal Remedy: Motherwort Tincture

Ingredients:

- 1 cup dried motherwort
- 2 cups vodka or brandy
- Glass jar with lid

Instructions:

1. **Prepare the Herb**: Measure out 1 cup of dried motherwort.

2. **Combine Ingredients**: Place the dried motherwort in a glass jar and cover with 2 cups of vodka or brandy.

3. **Seal and Store**: Seal the jar tightly and store it in a cool, dark place for 4-6 weeks, shaking it daily.

4. **Strain and Bottle**: After 4-6 weeks, strain the mixture through a cheesecloth into a clean glass bottle.

5. **Dosage**: Take 1 teaspoon of the tincture diluted in water up to three times a day.

Motherwort is known for its calming effects on the heart, helping to regulate heartbeat and reduce palpitations.

These herbal remedies, inspired by Barbara O'Neill's principles, provide natural support for managing cardiovascular ailments. By incorporating these remedies into your daily routine, along with maintaining a healthy diet and lifestyle, you can support your heart health and enhance your overall well-being. Always consult with a healthcare professional before starting any new treatment, especially if you have existing health conditions or are taking medications.

Exercise and Lifestyle Changes for a Healthy Heart

A healthy heart is essential for overall well-being. Regular exercise and lifestyle modifications play crucial roles in maintaining cardiovascular health. Barbara O'Neill emphasizes the importance of holistic approaches to heart health, combining natural remedies with healthy habits. This chapter explores specific exercise routines and lifestyle changes that can significantly enhance heart health, drawing inspiration from Barbara's teachings.

Importance of Regular Exercise

Exercise is vital for maintaining a healthy heart. It strengthens the heart muscle, improves blood circulation, lowers blood pressure, reduces cholesterol levels, and helps manage weight. Regular physical activity also alleviates stress and improves mood, which are important factors in heart health.

Types of Exercise for Heart Health

1. **Aerobic Exercise**

   o **Description**: Aerobic exercises, also known as cardio exercises, increase the heart rate and improve the efficiency of the cardiovascular system.

   o **Examples**: Walking, jogging, cycling, swimming, and dancing.

   o **Benefits**: Enhances heart and lung capacity, lowers blood pressure, and reduces the risk of heart disease.

   o **Recommended Frequency**: Aim for at least 150 minutes of moderate-intensity aerobic exercise per week or 75 minutes of vigorous-intensity exercise.

   o **Tips**: Start with a 30-minute brisk walk five days a week. Gradually increase the duration and intensity as your fitness improves.

2. **Strength Training**

   o **Description**: Strength training involves using resistance to build muscle mass and strength.

   o **Examples**: Weightlifting, resistance band exercises, and body-weight exercises like push-ups and squats.

   o **Benefits**: Increases muscle strength, improves metabolism, and supports healthy body weight.

- o **Recommended Frequency**: Include strength training exercises at least two days per week.

- o **Tips**: Begin with two 20-minute sessions per week, focusing on major muscle groups. Use light weights or resistance bands and gradually increase the resistance as you get stronger.

3. **Flexibility and Balance Exercises**

- o **Description**: These exercises enhance flexibility, improve balance, and reduce the risk of falls.

- o **Examples**: Yoga, Pilates, and stretching exercises.

- o **Benefits**: Improves range of motion, reduces muscle stiffness, and enhances overall physical performance.

- o **Recommended Frequency**: Perform flexibility and balance exercises daily or at least three times a week.

- o **Tips**: Incorporate a 10-minute stretching routine into your daily schedule. Try yoga classes or follow online videos that guide you through simple poses.

Incorporating Exercise into Daily Life

1. **Set Realistic Goals**: Start with small, achievable goals and gradually increase the intensity and duration of your workouts.

- o **Tips**: Use a fitness tracker to set and monitor goals, such as walking 5,000 steps per day and gradually increasing to 10,000 steps.

2. **Find Activities You Enjoy**: Choose exercises that you find enjoyable to make it easier to stick with your routine.

- o **Tips**: Experiment with different activities like dancing, swimming, or group fitness classes until you find one that you look forward to doing.

3. **Make it a Habit**: Schedule exercise sessions at the same time each day to create a consistent routine.

- o **Tips**: Set reminders on your phone or calendar to establish a regular workout schedule. Morning workouts can jumpstart your day, while evening sessions can help de-stress.

4. **Stay Active Throughout the Day**: Incorporate physical activity into your daily routine, such as taking the stairs instead of the elevator or walking during breaks.

- o **Tips**: Use a standing desk, take short walking breaks every hour, and opt for active commuting options like biking or walking.

Lifestyle Changes for Heart Health

1. **Healthy Diet**

    o **Focus on Whole Foods**: Consume a diet rich in fruits, vegetables, whole grains, lean proteins, and healthy fats.

    o **Tips**: Plan your meals ahead of time to ensure a balanced diet. Use a food diary to track your intake of whole foods versus processed foods.

    o **Limit Processed Foods**: Avoid foods high in refined sugars, trans fats, and sodium.

    o **Tips**: Read food labels carefully and prepare meals at home using fresh ingredients to control your intake of unhealthy additives.

    o **Herbal Supplements**: Consider incorporating heart-healthy herbs such as garlic, hawthorn, and turmeric into your diet.

    o **Tips**: Add fresh garlic to your cooking, brew hawthorn tea daily, and use turmeric in soups, stews, and smoothies.

2. **Manage Stress**

    o **Relaxation Techniques**: Practice meditation, deep breathing exercises, and yoga to manage stress effectively.

    o **Tips**: Dedicate 10-15 minutes each day to deep breathing exercises or guided meditation sessions. Apps like Calm or Headspace can be helpful.

    o **Prayer and Spiritual Practices**: Engage in regular prayer or spiritual practices, which Barbara O'Neill emphasizes as a means to achieve inner peace and reduce stress.

    o **Tips**: Set aside a quiet time each day for prayer or spiritual reflection. Create a peaceful space in your home for this purpose.

    o **Adequate Sleep**: Ensure you get 7-9 hours of quality sleep each night to support overall health and well-being.

    o **Tips**: Establish a bedtime routine that includes winding down activities such as reading, taking a warm bath, or listening to calming music.

3. **Avoid Harmful Habits**

    o **Quit Smoking**: Smoking is a major risk factor for heart disease. Seek support to quit smoking and avoid exposure to secondhand smoke.

- o **Tips**: Use nicotine replacement therapy, join a support group, or seek professional counseling to aid in quitting smoking.

- o **Limit Alcohol Consumption**: Drink alcohol in moderation, if at all. Excessive alcohol intake can lead to high blood pressure and other cardiovascular issues.

- o **Tips**: Limit alcohol intake to one drink per day for women and two for men. Substitute alcoholic beverages with healthier options like herbal teas or sparkling water with a splash of fruit juice.

4. **Regular Health Check-ups**

- o **Monitor Blood Pressure**: Keep track of your blood pressure levels and manage them through lifestyle changes and medication if necessary.

- o **Tips**: Purchase a home blood pressure monitor and check your readings regularly. Record them in a journal to share with your healthcare provider.

- o **Check Cholesterol Levels**: Regularly monitor your cholesterol levels and take steps to maintain healthy levels through diet and exercise.

- o **Tips**: Schedule annual check-ups with your doctor to monitor cholesterol levels. Follow a diet low in saturated fats and high in fiber to manage cholesterol.

- o **Stay Informed**: Stay updated with the latest information on heart health and consult with healthcare professionals for personalized advice.

- o **Tips**: Subscribe to reputable health newsletters or websites for updates on heart health. Attend health seminars or workshops to learn more.

Holistic Approaches to Heart Health

1. **Herbal Remedies**

- o **Garlic**: Known for its blood-thinning properties, garlic can help lower blood pressure and cholesterol levels.

- o **Tips**: Consume one to two raw garlic cloves daily. If the taste is too strong, consider garlic supplements after consulting a healthcare provider.

- o **Hawthorn**: This herb improves blood circulation and strengthens the heart muscle.

- o **Tips**: Brew hawthorn tea by steeping one teaspoon of dried hawthorn berries in hot water for 10 minutes. Drink two to three cups daily.

- o **Turmeric**: With its anti-inflammatory properties, turmeric supports heart health by reducing inflammation and oxidative stress.

- o **Tips**: Add one teaspoon of turmeric powder to smoothies, soups, or stews daily. You can also take turmeric supplements after consulting a healthcare provider.

2. **Emotional and Social Well-being**

   o **Social Connections**: Maintain strong relationships with family and friends to foster emotional well-being.

   o **Tips**: Schedule regular social activities, such as family dinners, coffee with friends, or joining community groups.

   o **Positive Mindset**: Cultivate a positive outlook on life and practice gratitude to enhance mental health.

   o **Tips**: Keep a gratitude journal and write down three things you are thankful for each day. Engage in positive self-talk and surround yourself with uplifting influences.

Exercise and lifestyle changes are foundational to maintaining a healthy heart. By integrating regular physical activity, adopting a heart-healthy diet, managing stress, avoiding harmful habits, and embracing holistic approaches, you can significantly enhance your cardiovascular health. These strategies offer a comprehensive approach to achieving and maintaining a healthy heart, empowering you to live a vibrant and fulfilling life.

Chapter 7: Managing Diabetes

Understanding Blood Sugar Control

Understanding Blood Sugar Control

Diabetes is a chronic condition that affects millions of people worldwide. It requires careful management of blood sugar levels to prevent complications and maintain overall health. Understanding the mechanisms of blood sugar control and implementing natural strategies can empower individuals to take charge of their health.

The Basics of Blood Sugar

Blood sugar, or glucose, is the primary source of energy for the body's cells. It is derived from the carbohydrates we consume and is transported to cells via the bloodstream. Insulin, a hormone produced by the pancreas, facilitates the uptake of glucose into cells, where it is used for energy.

In diabetes, the body either does not produce enough insulin (Type 1 diabetes) or becomes resistant to insulin's effects (Type 2 diabetes). This leads to elevated blood sugar levels, which, if unmanaged, can cause serious health issues.

The Role of Insulin

Insulin is crucial for regulating blood sugar levels. After eating, carbohydrates are broken down into glucose, causing blood sugar levels to rise. In response, the pancreas releases insulin, which helps cells absorb glucose, reducing blood sugar levels. In people with diabetes, this process is impaired.

Key Factors Affecting Blood Sugar Control

1. **Diet**

   o **Carbohydrate Intake**: The type and amount of carbohydrates consumed significantly impact blood sugar levels. Simple carbohydrates (sugars) cause rapid spikes, whereas complex carbohydrates (whole grains, vegetables) are digested more slowly, leading to gradual increases.

   o **Glycemic Index**: Foods with a low glycemic index (GI) have a slower impact on blood sugar levels compared to high GI foods. Choosing low GI foods helps maintain stable blood sugar levels.

2. **Physical Activity**

- **Exercise**: Physical activity increases insulin sensitivity, allowing cells to use glucose more effectively. Regular exercise can lower blood sugar levels and improve overall health.

- **Types of Exercise**: Both aerobic exercises (like walking, swimming) and resistance training (like weight lifting) are beneficial for blood sugar control.

3. **Stress**

- **Impact on Blood Sugar**: Stress triggers the release of hormones like cortisol, which can raise blood sugar levels. Managing stress through relaxation techniques, mindfulness, and physical activity is essential.

- **Barbara's Insight**: Barbara O'Neill emphasizes the importance of a balanced lifestyle that includes stress management to support overall health and blood sugar control.

4. **Sleep**

- **Sleep Quality**: Poor sleep can affect hormone levels, including insulin, leading to impaired blood sugar control. Aim for 7-9 hours of quality sleep per night.

- **Sleep Hygiene**: Establishing a regular sleep routine and creating a restful environment can improve sleep quality.

5. **Hydration**

- **Water Intake**: Staying hydrated helps the kidneys flush out excess sugar through urine. Drinking plenty of water is essential for managing blood sugar levels.

Natural Strategies for Blood Sugar Control

1. **Dietary Adjustments**

- **Balanced Meals**: Incorporate a balance of carbohydrates, proteins, and healthy fats in every meal. This helps slow the absorption of glucose and prevents spikes in blood sugar.

- **Fiber-Rich Foods**: Foods high in fiber, such as vegetables, fruits, legumes, and whole grains, slow down the digestion and absorption of carbohydrates.

- **Healthy Fats**: Include sources of healthy fats like avocados, nuts, seeds, and olive oil to improve insulin sensitivity.

2. **Herbal Remedies**

- **Bitter Melon (Momordica charantia)**: Known for its blood sugar-lowering properties. Can be consumed as a juice or supplement.

- o **Fenugreek (Trigonella foenum-graecum)**: Contains soluble fiber that helps control blood sugar levels. Fenugreek seeds can be soaked overnight and consumed on an empty stomach.

  - o **Cinnamon (Cinnamomum verum)**: Has been shown to improve insulin sensitivity. Add cinnamon to meals, smoothies, or teas.

3. **Physical Activity**

  - o **Regular Exercise**: Engage in at least 30 minutes of moderate exercise most days of the week. This could include walking, cycling, swimming, or strength training.

  - o **Daily Movement**: Incorporate more physical activity into daily routines, such as taking the stairs, walking during breaks, or gardening.

4. **Stress Management**

  - o **Mindfulness and Meditation**: Practices like mindfulness and meditation can reduce stress and its impact on blood sugar levels.

  - o **Relaxation Techniques**: Techniques such as deep breathing, yoga, and tai chi can help manage stress effectively.

5. **Regular Monitoring**

  - o **Blood Sugar Levels**: Regularly monitor blood sugar levels to understand how different foods, activities, and stress affect your blood sugar. This can help in making informed decisions about diet and lifestyle.

By understanding the mechanisms of blood sugar control and incorporating these natural strategies, individuals with diabetes can manage their condition more effectively. Holistic approach emphasizes the importance of a balanced diet, regular physical activity, stress management, and the use of natural remedies to support overall health and well-being.

Natural Supplements and Herbs for Diabetes

Managing diabetes naturally involves incorporating specific herbs and supplements known for their blood sugar-lowering properties. These remedies can be used alongside conventional treatments, with a focus on achieving better blood sugar control and improving overall health. Here are some effective natural supplements and herbs for managing diabetes, including detailed preparation methods and dosages.

1. Bitter Melon (Momordica charantia)

Key Constituents and Properties

Bitter melon contains charantin, vicine, and polypeptide-p, which mimic insulin and help lower blood sugar levels. It also has antioxidant properties that protect against cellular damage.

Different Uses Against Diseases

Bitter melon is effective in reducing blood sugar levels and improving glucose tolerance. It can also help manage weight, a critical factor in diabetes management.

Preparation Methods

- **Bitter Melon Juice:**
    - Ingredients: 1-2 bitter melons
    - Instructions: Wash the bitter melons thoroughly. Remove the seeds and blend the flesh. Strain the mixture to extract the juice. Consume 50-100 ml of bitter melon juice on an empty stomach daily.

- **Bitter Melon Stir-fry:**
    - Ingredients: 1-2 bitter melons, 1 tbsp olive oil, salt to taste
    - Instructions: Slice the bitter melons thinly. Heat olive oil in a pan, add the slices, and stir-fry until they are soft. Season with salt. Consume as part of a meal.

Dosage, Safety, and Precautions

- Dosage: 50-100 ml of juice daily or 1-2 servings of cooked bitter melon.

- Safety: Consult a healthcare provider before use, especially if pregnant or breastfeeding. May cause hypoglycemia if taken with other blood sugar-lowering medications.

2. Fenugreek (Trigonella foenum-graecum)

Key Constituents and Properties

Fenugreek seeds contain soluble fiber, saponins, and alkaloids that help manage blood sugar levels by slowing down carbohydrate absorption and improving insulin sensitivity.

Different Uses Against Diseases

Fenugreek is effective in lowering blood sugar levels and improving lipid profiles. It also helps with appetite control and digestion.

Preparation Methods

- **Soaked Fenugreek Seeds:**
    - Ingredients: 2 tbsp fenugreek seeds, 1 cup water
    - Instructions: Soak fenugreek seeds in water overnight. In the morning, consume the seeds and water on an empty stomach.
- **Fenugreek Tea:**
    - Ingredients: 1 tsp fenugreek seeds, 1 cup boiling water
    - Instructions: Crush the fenugreek seeds and add them to boiling water. Let it steep for 10 minutes. Strain and drink once or twice daily.

Dosage, Safety, and Precautions

- Dosage: 2 tbsp of soaked seeds daily or 1-2 cups of fenugreek tea.
- Safety: Generally safe but may cause gastrointestinal upset in some individuals. Not recommended for pregnant women due to its uterine-stimulating effects.

3. Cinnamon (Cinnamomum verum)

Key Constituents and Properties

Cinnamon contains cinnamaldehyde, polyphenols, and flavonoids that improve insulin sensitivity and have antioxidant and anti-inflammatory properties.

Different Uses Against Diseases

Cinnamon helps lower fasting blood sugar levels, reduce hemoglobin A1c, and improve lipid profiles.

Preparation Methods

- **Cinnamon Tea:**
    - Ingredients: 1 tsp ground cinnamon or 1 cinnamon stick, 1 cup boiling water
    - Instructions: Add cinnamon to boiling water and let it steep for 10-15 minutes. Strain and drink once or twice daily.

- **Cinnamon Smoothie:**
    - Ingredients: 1 banana, 1 cup almond milk, 1 tsp ground cinnamon, 1 tbsp honey
    - Instructions: Blend all ingredients until smooth. Enjoy as a nutritious breakfast or snack.

Dosage, Safety, and Precautions

- Dosage: 1-2 tsp of ground cinnamon daily or 1-2 cups of cinnamon tea.

- Safety: High doses may cause liver toxicity due to coumarin content. Use Ceylon cinnamon for lower coumarin levels. Consult a healthcare provider if on blood-thinning medication.

4. Ginseng (Panax ginseng)

Key Constituents and Properties

Ginseng contains ginsenosides that help improve insulin production, enhance glucose uptake, and reduce oxidative stress.

Different Uses Against Diseases

Ginseng is effective in reducing fasting blood sugar levels and improving insulin sensitivity. It also boosts energy and reduces fatigue.

Preparation Methods

- **Ginseng Tea:**
  - Ingredients: 1 g dried ginseng root, 1 cup boiling water
  - Instructions: Add dried ginseng root to boiling water and let it steep for 5-10 minutes. Strain and drink once daily.

- **Ginseng Capsules:**
  - Ingredients: Dried ginseng root, empty capsules
  - Instructions: Grind dried ginseng root into a powder. Fill capsules with the powder and take as directed by a healthcare provider.

Dosage, Safety, and Precautions

- Dosage: 1-2 g of dried root daily or as directed for capsules.
- Safety: May cause insomnia or jitteriness in some individuals. Avoid using for extended periods without breaks. Consult a healthcare provider if pregnant or on medication.

5. Gymnema Sylvestre (Gymnema sylvestre)

Key Constituents and Properties

Gymnema contains gymnemic acids that block sugar absorption in the intestines and enhance insulin secretion.

Different Uses Against Diseases

Gymnema is effective in reducing sugar cravings, lowering blood sugar levels, and improving lipid profiles.

Preparation Methods

- **Gymnema Tea:**
  - Ingredients: 1 tsp dried gymnema leaves, 1 cup boiling water
  - Instructions: Add dried gymnema leaves to boiling water and let it steep for 5-10 minutes. Strain and drink once daily.

- **Gymnema Powder:**
  - Ingredients: Dried gymnema leaves
  - Instructions: Grind dried gymnema leaves into a powder. Add 1 tsp of the powder to smoothies, juices, or water.

Dosage, Safety, and Precautions

- Dosage: 1 tsp of dried leaves daily or as directed for powder.
- Safety: Generally safe but may cause mild gastrointestinal upset. Consult a healthcare provider if on diabetes medication to avoid hypoglycemia.

Additional Herbal Remedies for Diabetes

6. Bilberry (Vaccinium myrtillus)

- **Key Constituents and Properties**: Contains anthocyanins, which improve blood sugar control and protect against oxidative stress.
- **Preparation**: Use dried bilberries to make tea or take as a supplement. To make tea, add 1-2 tsp of dried bilberries to boiling water, steep for 10 minutes, and strain. Drink once daily.
- **Dosage, Safety, and Precautions**: 1-2 tsp of dried bilberries daily. Generally safe, but consult a healthcare provider if on anticoagulant medication.

7. Aloe Vera (Aloe barbadensis)

- **Key Constituents and Properties**: Contains glucomannan and aloin, which help lower blood sugar levels and improve insulin sensitivity.
- **Preparation**: Extract fresh aloe vera gel and blend with water or juice. Consume 1-2 tbsp daily.
- **Dosage, Safety, and Precautions**: 1-2 tbsp of aloe vera gel daily. May cause gastrointestinal upset in some individuals. Consult a healthcare provider if pregnant or breastfeeding.

8. Holy Basil (Ocimum sanctum)

- **Key Constituents and Properties**: Contains eugenol, caryophyllene, and triterpenoids, which improve insulin sensitivity and lower blood sugar levels.

- **Preparation**: Use fresh or dried leaves to make tea. Add 1-2 tsp of leaves to boiling water, steep for 5-10 minutes, and strain. Drink once or twice daily.

- **Dosage, Safety, and Precautions**: 1-2 cups of tea daily. Generally safe but may cause mild side effects in some individuals.

9. Neem (Azadirachta indica)

- **Key Constituents and Properties**: Contains nimbin, nimbidin, and quercetin, which help lower blood sugar levels and improve insulin sensitivity.

- **Preparation**: Use fresh or dried neem leaves to make tea. Add 1 tsp of leaves to boiling water, steep for 5-10 minutes, and strain. Drink once daily.

- **Dosage, Safety, and Precautions**: 1 cup of tea daily. Consult a healthcare provider if pregnant or breastfeeding.

10. Prickly Pear (Opuntia ficus-indica)

- **Key Constituents and Properties**: Contains pectin and fiber, which help lower blood sugar levels and improve insulin sensitivity.

- **Preparation**: Consume fresh prickly pear pads or juice. For juice, blend the pads and strain the mixture.

- **Dosage, Safety, and Precautions**: 1 cup of juice or 1 pad daily. Generally safe but may cause mild gastrointestinal upset in some individuals.

Incorporating these natural supplements and herbs into a balanced diet and healthy lifestyle can significantly aid in managing diabetes. ombining natural remedies with proper nutrition, physical activity, stress management, and regular monitoring to achieve optimal blood sugar control and overall well-being. Always consult a healthcare provider before starting any new supplement or herbal regimen, especially if you are currently on medication or have other health conditions.

Dietary and Lifestyle Changes

Managing diabetes effectively requires a combination of dietary modifications and lifestyle changes. By embracing a holistic approach, you can help regulate blood sugar levels, reduce the risk of complications, and improve overall health. Here are some comprehensive strategies, inspired by Barbara O'Neill's teachings, to manage diabetes through diet and lifestyle.

Dietary Changes

1. Embrace a Low Glycemic Index (GI) Diet

Foods with a low glycemic index (GI) release glucose more slowly and steadily, helping to maintain stable blood sugar levels. Incorporate the following low-GI foods into your diet:

- **Non-Starchy Vegetables**: Leafy greens, broccoli, cauliflower, zucchini, and bell peppers.

- **Whole Grains**: Quinoa, barley, steel-cut oats, and brown rice.

- **Legumes**: Lentils, chickpeas, black beans, and kidney beans.

- **Fruits**: Berries, cherries, apples, and pears (in moderation).

2. Increase Fiber Intake

Fiber slows down the absorption of sugar and improves blood sugar control. Aim to include at least 25-30 grams of fiber daily from sources such as:

- **Vegetables**: Brussels sprouts, carrots, and artichokes.

- **Fruits**: Avocados, raspberries, and oranges.

- **Whole Grains**: Oats, flaxseeds, and chia seeds.

- **Legumes**: Lentils, black beans, and split peas.

3. Choose Healthy Fats

Healthy fats can improve insulin sensitivity and reduce inflammation. Include these healthy fats in your diet:

- **Nuts and Seeds**: Almonds, walnuts, chia seeds, and flaxseeds.

- **Oils**: Extra virgin olive oil, coconut oil, and avocado oil.

- **Fish**: Salmon, mackerel, sardines, and other fatty fish high in omega-3 fatty acids.

4. Opt for Lean Protein Sources

Protein helps stabilize blood sugar levels and promotes satiety. Choose lean protein sources such as:

- **Poultry**: Skinless chicken and turkey.
- **Fish**: Salmon, tuna, and trout.
- **Plant-Based Proteins**: Tofu, tempeh, edamame, and lentils.

5. Avoid Processed and Sugary Foods

Limit or eliminate foods that can spike blood sugar levels, such as:

- **Sugary Beverages**: Sodas, fruit juices, and energy drinks.
- **Refined Carbohydrates**: White bread, pastries, and pasta.
- **Processed Snacks**: Chips, cookies, and candies.

Lifestyle Changes

1. Regular Physical Activity

Exercise enhances insulin sensitivity and helps lower blood sugar levels. Aim for at least 150 minutes of moderate-intensity aerobic exercise per week, such as:

- **Walking**: A brisk 30-minute walk five times a week.
- **Cycling**: Riding a bike around your neighborhood or on a stationary bike.
- **Swimming**: Engaging in lap swimming or water aerobics.

Incorporate strength training exercises, such as weightlifting or resistance band exercises, two to three times a week to build muscle mass and further improve insulin sensitivity.

2. Maintain a Healthy Weight

Achieving and maintaining a healthy weight can significantly improve blood sugar control. Focus on:

- **Balanced Diet**: Follow a diet rich in whole foods, healthy fats, and lean proteins.

- **Regular Exercise**: Combine aerobic activities with strength training.

- **Mindful Eating**: Pay attention to hunger and fullness cues, and avoid emotional eating.

3. Stress Management

Chronic stress can lead to elevated blood sugar levels. Implement stress-reducing practices such as:

- **Mindfulness and Meditation**: Practice mindfulness meditation or deep-breathing exercises daily.

- **Yoga**: Engage in yoga sessions to promote relaxation and improve flexibility.

- **Adequate Sleep**: Ensure you get 7-9 hours of quality sleep each night to reduce stress and improve overall health.

4. Regular Monitoring

Keep track of your blood sugar levels to understand how your body responds to different foods, activities, and stressors. Use a glucose meter to monitor your levels regularly and adjust your diet and lifestyle accordingly.

5. Hydration

Proper hydration is crucial for maintaining blood sugar balance. Aim to drink at least eight 8-ounce glasses of water daily. Adequate hydration helps kidneys flush out excess glucose through urine.

Managing diabetes requires a multifaceted approach that combines dietary modifications, regular physical activity, stress management, and natural remedies. By following these comprehensive strategies and integrating them into your daily routine, you can achieve better blood sugar control, reduce the risk of complications, and improve your overall quality of life. Always consult a healthcare provider before making significant changes to your diet, exercise, or medication regimen, especially when incorporating herbal remedies.

Chapter 8: Women's Health

Natural Approaches to Hormonal Balance

Hormonal balance is vital for overall health and well-being, particularly for women. Hormones regulate numerous bodily functions, including metabolism, mood, and reproductive health. An imbalance can lead to various health issues, such as irregular menstrual cycles, infertility, and menopause symptoms. Here are some natural approaches to maintaining hormonal balance.

1. Nutrient-Rich Diet

A balanced diet rich in essential nutrients can help regulate hormone production and function. Incorporate the following foods into your diet:

- **Healthy Fats**: Avocados, nuts, seeds, and olive oil provide essential fatty acids needed for hormone production.

- **Leafy Greens**: Spinach, kale, and broccoli are high in vitamins and minerals that support endocrine function.

- **Whole Grains**: Brown rice, quinoa, and oats help stabilize blood sugar levels, which is crucial for hormonal balance.

- **Lean Proteins**: Fish, chicken, and plant-based proteins support tissue repair and hormone production.

2. Herbal Remedies

Certain herbs are known for their hormone-balancing properties. Integrate these herbs into your daily routine to support hormonal health:

- **Maca Root (Lepidium meyenii)**: Known for its ability to balance hormones and improve fertility. Maca can be consumed as a powder added to smoothies or oatmeal.

- **Chaste Tree Berry (Vitex agnus-castus)**: Helps regulate menstrual cycles and alleviate PMS symptoms. This herb is often taken as a tincture or capsule.

- **Black Cohosh (Actaea racemosa)**: Effective in reducing menopausal symptoms like hot flashes and mood swings. Typically consumed as a tea or supplement.

- **Evening Primrose Oil (Oenothera biennis)**: Rich in gamma-linolenic acid (GLA), which helps balance hormones and reduce PMS symptoms. It can be taken in capsule form.

3. Stress Management

Chronic stress can lead to hormonal imbalances by increasing cortisol levels, which can interfere with other hormone functions. Implement these stress-reducing practices:

- **Mindfulness and Meditation**: Practice mindfulness meditation or deep-breathing exercises daily to reduce stress and promote relaxation.

- **Yoga**: Engage in yoga sessions to balance the body and mind, improve flexibility, and reduce stress.

- **Adequate Sleep**: Ensure you get 7-9 hours of quality sleep each night to support overall health and hormonal balance.

4. Regular Physical Activity

Exercise helps regulate hormones, improve insulin sensitivity, and reduce stress. Aim for a mix of aerobic exercises, strength training, and flexibility exercises:

- **Aerobic Exercises**: Walking, running, and swimming can boost your metabolism and improve cardiovascular health.

- **Strength Training**: Weight lifting and resistance band exercises build muscle mass and support metabolic health.

- **Flexibility Exercises**: Yoga and stretching enhance flexibility and reduce stress.

5. Avoid Endocrine Disruptors

Endocrine disruptors are chemicals that can interfere with hormone function. Reduce your exposure to these chemicals by:

- **Using Natural Products**: Choose natural skincare and cleaning products free from parabens, phthalates, and other harmful chemicals.

- **Avoiding Plastic Containers**: Use glass or stainless steel containers instead of plastic to store food and beverages.

- **Eating Organic**: Choose organic produce to reduce exposure to pesticides and herbicides that can act as endocrine disruptors.

6. Hydration

Staying hydrated is crucial for overall health and hormonal balance. Drink at least eight 8-ounce glasses of water daily to support bodily functions and maintain optimal health.

7. Supplementation

Certain supplements can support hormonal health. Consider these supplements under the guidance of a healthcare professional:

- **Vitamin D**: Supports immune function and hormonal balance. Spend time in the sunlight or take a supplement if necessary.

- **Magnesium**: Helps reduce stress and support sleep, both of which are crucial for hormonal health.

- **Omega-3 Fatty Acids**: Found in fish oil or flaxseed oil, omega-3s support overall health and reduce inflammation.

Maintaining hormonal balance is essential for women's health and well-being. By following these natural approaches, including a nutrient-rich diet, herbal remedies, stress management, regular physical activity, and avoiding endocrine disruptors, you can support your hormonal health and improve your overall quality of life. Always consult with a healthcare professional before starting any new supplements or making significant changes to your health routine.

Herbs for Reproductive Health

Reproductive health is a crucial aspect of overall well-being, especially for women. Herbs have been used for centuries to support reproductive health, alleviate symptoms associated with menstrual cycles, and enhance fertility. This section delves into various herbs that can help maintain and improve reproductive health. Remember to consult with a healthcare professional before starting any new herbal regimen.

1. Chaste Tree (Vitex agnus-castus)

- **Overview**: Chaste tree, also known as Vitex, is one of the most renowned herbs for female reproductive health. It helps regulate menstrual cycles and alleviate symptoms of premenstrual syndrome (PMS).

- **Active Compounds**: Flavonoids, iridoid glycosides (agnuside), essential oils.

- **Uses**:

  o Regulates menstrual cycles

  o Reduces PMS symptoms such as mood swings, bloating, and breast tenderness o   Supports fertility by balancing hormones

- **Preparation**: Chaste tree is commonly taken as a tincture or capsule. For tinctures, follow the instructions on the bottle. For capsules, typically 400-500 mg per day is recommended.

- **Safety and Precautions**: Generally safe for most women, but it may interact with hormone therapies. Avoid during pregnancy unless advised by a healthcare provider.

2. Red Raspberry Leaf (Rubus idaeus)

- **Overview**: Red raspberry leaf is well-known for its benefits to the reproductive system, especially during pregnancy. It strengthens the uterine muscles and supports overall reproductive health.

- **Active Compounds**: Tannins, flavonoids, vitamins (A, B, C, E), minerals (calcium, iron, magnesium).

- **Uses**:

    o   Strengthens and tones the uterus

    o   Eases menstrual cramps and heavy bleeding

    o   Supports a healthy pregnancy and eases labor

- **Preparation**: Make a tea by steeping 1-2 teaspoons of dried leaves in hot water for 10-15 minutes. Drink 2-3 cups daily.

- **Safety and Precautions**: Safe for most women, but consult a healthcare provider if pregnant or breastfeeding.

3. Dong Quai (Angelica sinensis)

- **Overview**: Dong Quai, also known as "female ginseng," is used to balance hormones and alleviate menstrual discomfort.

- **Active Compounds**: Ferulic acid, polysaccharides, coumarins.

- **Uses**:

    o   Balances hormones and alleviates PMS symptoms

    o   Improves blood flow and reduces menstrual cramps

    o   Supports overall reproductive health

- **Preparation**: Commonly taken as a tincture, capsule, or decoction. For a decoction, simmer 1-2 teaspoons of dried root in water for 20-30 minutes. Drink 1-2 cups daily.

- **Safety and Precautions**: Avoid during pregnancy and breastfeeding. May interact with blood-thinning medications.

4. Black Cohosh (Actaea racemosa)

- **Overview**: Black Cohosh is frequently used to alleviate menopausal symptoms and support overall reproductive health.

- **Active Compounds**: Triterpene glycosides (actein), isoflavones, tannins.

- **Uses**:

    o Reduces menopausal symptoms like hot flashes and night sweats

    o Alleviates menstrual cramps and PMS symptoms

    o Supports hormonal balance

- **Preparation**: Available as a tincture, capsule, or tea. For tea, steep 1 teaspoon of dried root in hot water for 10-15 minutes. Drink 1-2 cups daily.

- **Safety and Precautions**: Generally safe for short-term use. Avoid during pregnancy. Consult with a healthcare provider if on hormone replacement therapy or with liver conditions.

5. Maca Root (Lepidium meyenii)

- **Overview**: Maca root is known for its ability to enhance fertility and balance hormones.

- **Active Compounds**: Macamides, glucosinolates, polyphenols.

- **Uses**:

    o Balances hormones and boosts fertility

    o Increases energy and stamina

    o Alleviates symptoms of PMS and menopause

- **Preparation**: Maca is commonly available as a powder or capsule. Add 1-2 teaspoons of maca powder to smoothies, oatmeal, or yogurt daily.

- **Safety and Precautions**: Generally safe for most people. Start with a small dose to assess tolerance. Avoid during pregnancy and breastfeeding without medical advice.

6. Evening Primrose Oil (Oenothera biennis)

- **Overview**: Evening Primrose Oil is rich in gamma-linolenic acid (GLA), which helps balance hormones and reduce PMS symptoms.

- **Active Compounds**: Gamma-linolenic acid (GLA), linoleic acid.

- **Uses**:
    - Alleviates PMS symptoms like breast tenderness and mood swings
    - Supports skin health
    - Balances hormones

- **Preparation**: Typically taken in capsule form, with a common dose being 500 mg 2-3 times daily.

- **Safety and Precautions**: Generally safe for most women. Consult with a healthcare provider if on blood-thinning medications.

7. Nettle (Urtica dioica)

- **Overview**: Nettle is highly nutritious and supports overall reproductive health.

- **Active Compounds**: Vitamins (A, C, K), minerals (iron, calcium, magnesium), flavonoids.

- **Uses**:
    - Reduces heavy menstrual bleeding
    - Supports fertility by providing essential nutrients
    - Alleviates PMS symptoms

- **Preparation**: Make a tea by steeping 1-2 teaspoons of dried nettle leaves in hot water for 10-15 minutes. Drink 2-3 cups daily.

- **Safety and Precautions**: Generally safe for most people. Avoid if allergic to nettle. Consult with a healthcare provider if pregnant or breastfeeding.

8. Ashwagandha (Withania somnifera)

- **Overview**: Ashwagandha is an adaptogen that helps the body cope with stress and supports hormonal balance.

- **Active Compounds**: Withanolides, alkaloids, saponins.

- **Uses**:
  - Balances hormones and reduces stress
  - Supports reproductive health and fertility
  - Enhances energy and stamina
- **Preparation**: Commonly taken as a powder or capsule. Add 1-2 teaspoons of ashwagandha powder to smoothies, milk, or warm water daily.
- **Safety and Precautions**: Generally safe for most people. Consult with a healthcare provider if pregnant, breastfeeding, or on medication.

9. Vitex (Vitex agnus-castus)

- **Overview**: Vitex is commonly used to treat PMS, menopause symptoms, and other hormone-related issues.
- **Active Compounds**: Iridoid glycosides, flavonoids, essential oils.
- **Uses**:
  - Regulates menstrual cycles and alleviates PMS symptoms
  - Reduces menopausal symptoms
  - Supports fertility by balancing hormones
- **Preparation**: Available as a tincture or capsule. For tinctures, follow the instructions on the bottle. For capsules, typically 400-500 mg per day is recommended.
- **Safety and Precautions**: Generally safe for most women. Avoid during pregnancy unless advised by a healthcare provider. May interact with hormone therapies.

10. Shatavari (Asparagus racemosus)

- **Overview**: Shatavari is an adaptogenic herb known for its ability to support female reproductive health.
- **Active Compounds**: Saponins (shatavarins), alkaloids, flavonoids.
- **Uses**:
  - Balances hormones and enhances fertility
  - Reduces menopausal symptoms
  - Supports overall reproductive health

- **Preparation**: Commonly taken as a powder or capsule. Add 1-2 teaspoons of shatavari powder to smoothies, milk, or warm water daily.

- **Safety and Precautions**: Generally safe for most people. Consult with a healthcare provider if pregnant, breastfeeding, or on medication.

Incorporating these herbs into your daily routine can support and enhance your reproductive health. Each herb offers unique benefits and can be used to address specific reproductive health issues. Always consult with a healthcare professional before starting any new herbal regimen, especially if you are pregnant, breastfeeding, or on medication. Embrace these natural remedies to support your reproductive health and overall well-being, inspired by the teachings of Barbara

Managing Menstrual and Menopausal Symptoms

Menstrual and menopausal symptoms can significantly impact a woman's quality of life. However, natural remedies and lifestyle adjustments, can offer relief and help manage these symptoms effectively. This chapter delves into various strategies, including herbal remedies, dietary changes, and holistic practices to manage menstrual and menopausal symptoms.

Common Menstrual Symptoms

- **Dysmenorrhea (Menstrual Cramps)**

- **Premenstrual Syndrome (PMS)**

- **Heavy Menstrual Bleeding (Menorrhagia)**

- **Mood Swings and Irritability**

- **Bloating and Water Retention**

Herbal Remedies for Menstrual Symptoms

1. **Ginger (Zingiber officinale)**

   o **Overview**: Ginger is known for its anti-inflammatory and pain-relieving properties.

   o **Uses**: Relieves menstrual cramps and reduces inflammation.

   o **Preparation**:

      - **Ginger Tea**: Slice a few pieces of fresh ginger and steep in hot water for 10-15 minutes. Drink 2-3 cups daily during your menstrual cycle.

- o **Safety and Precautions**: Generally safe. Consult a healthcare provider if pregnant or on blood-thinning medications.

2. **Chamomile (Matricaria recutita)**

   - o **Overview**: Chamomile is calming and can help reduce cramps and improve mood.

   - o **Uses**: Alleviates menstrual cramps and reduces anxiety.

   - o **Preparation**:

     - **Chamomile Tea**: Steep 1-2 teaspoons of dried chamomile flowers in hot water for 10 minutes. Drink 2-3 cups daily.

   - o **Safety and Precautions**: Generally safe. Avoid if allergic to ragweed.

3. **Chaste Tree (Vitex agnus-castus)**

   - o **Overview**: Helps balance hormones and reduce PMS symptoms.

   - o **Uses**: Alleviates breast tenderness, mood swings, and bloating.

   - o **Preparation**:

     - **Vitex Tincture**: Follow the instructions on the tincture bottle. Generally, 20-40 drops daily in water or juice.

   - o **Safety and Precautions**: Avoid during pregnancy. Consult with a healthcare provider if on hormone therapies.

4. **Evening Primrose Oil (Oenothera biennis)**

   - o **Overview**: Rich in gamma-linolenic acid (GLA), it helps balance hormones.

   - o **Uses**: Reduces breast tenderness and PMS symptoms.

   - o **Preparation**:

     - **Capsules**: Typically, 500 mg 2-3 times daily.

   - o **Safety and Precautions**: Consult with a healthcare provider if on blood-thinning medications.

Dietary and Lifestyle Tips for M_____ Health

1. **Maintain a Balanced D**

   - o **Focus on whol**_____ rate plenty of fruits, vegetables, whole grains, and lean proteins.

   - o **Avoid proce**_____ ke of processed and sugary foods that can exacerbate symptoms

2. **Stay Hydrate**

o **Drink plenty of water**: Helps reduce bloating and supports overall health.

3. **Regular Exercise**

    o **Engage in physical activity**: Regular exercise can help reduce the severity of cramps and improve mood.

4. **Stress Management**

    o **Practice relaxation techniques**: Yoga, meditation, and deep breathing can help manage stress and reduce PMS symptoms.

Menopausal Symptoms Management

Common Menopausal Symptoms

- **Hot Flashes and Night Sweats**
- **Mood Swings and Irritability**
- **Vaginal Dryness**
- **Sleep Disturbances**
- **Weight Gain**

Herbal Remedies for Menopausal Symptoms

1. **Black Cohosh (Actaea racemosa)**

    o **Overview**: Commonly used to reduce hot flashes and night sweats.

    o **Uses**: Alleviates hot flashes, night sweats, and mood swings.

    o **Preparation**:

      ▪ **Black Cohosh Tea**: Steep 1 teaspoon of dried root in hot water for 10-15 minutes. Drink 1-2 cups daily.

    o **Safety and Precautions**: Avoid during pregnancy. Consult with a healthcare provider if on hormone therapies or with liver conditions.

2. **Red Clover (Trifolium pratense)**

    o **Overview**: Contains phytoestrogens that help balance hormones.

    o **Uses**: Reduces hot flashes and improves bone health.

- o **Preparation:**

    - **Red Clover Tea:** Steep 1-2 teaspoons of dried flowers in hot water for 10-15 minutes. Drink 2-3 cups daily.

- o **Safety and Precautions:** Generally safe. Consult a healthcare provider if on blood-thinning medications.

3. **Sage (Salvia officinalis)**

    - o **Overview:** Effective in reducing hot flashes and night sweats.

    - o **Uses:** Reduces hot flashes and night sweats.

    - o **Preparation:**

        - **Sage Tea:** Steep 1-2 teaspoons of dried leaves in hot water for 10 minutes. Drink 1-2 cups daily.

    - o **Safety and Precautions:** Avoid during pregnancy and breastfeeding. Consult a healthcare provider if on medications.

4. **Maca (Lepidium meyenii)**

    - o **Overview:** An adaptogen that supports hormonal balance.

    - o **Uses:** Reduces menopausal symptoms and increases energy.

    - o **Preparation:**

        - **Maca Powder:** Add 1-2 teaspoons to smoothies, yogurt, or oatmeal daily.

    - o **Safety and Precautions:** Generally safe. Start with a small dose to assess tolerance.

Dietary and Lifestyle Tips for Menopausal Health

1. **Adopt a Healthy Diet**

    - o **Focus on nutrient-dense foods:** Incorporate plenty of fruits, vegetables, whole grains, and lean proteins.

    - o **Include phytoestrogens:** Foods like soy, flaxseed, and legumes can help balance hormones.

2. **Stay Hydrated**

    - o **Drink plenty of water:** Helps reduce hot flashes and maintain overall health.

3. **Exercise Regularly**

    - o **Engage in physical activity:** Regular exercise can help manage weight, improve mood, and reduce symptoms.

4. **Practice Stress Management**

   o **Incorporate relaxation techniques**: Yoga, meditation, and deep breathing can help manage stress and reduce symptoms.

5. **Ensure Adequate Sleep**

   o **Establish a regular sleep routine**: Aim for 7-8 hours of sleep per night. Create a calming bedtime routine to improve sleep quality.

6. **Stay Connected**

   o **Maintain social connections**: Support from friends, family, and community can help manage emotional changes during menopause.

Managing menstrual and menopausal symptoms naturally can greatly enhance your quality of life. By incorporating herbal remedies, maintaining a balanced diet, staying hydrated, exercising regularly, and managing stress, you can effectively manage these symptoms. Always consult with a healthcare professional before starting any new herbal regimen, especially if you are pregnant, breastfeeding, or on medication. Embrace these natural remedies and lifestyle tips to support your reproductive health and overall well-being.

Chapter 9: Skin Health and Beauty

Natural Treatments for Common Skin Conditions

Our skin, the largest organ of the body, is a reflection of our internal health. Common skin conditions such as acne, eczema, psoriasis, and dry skin can often be managed and alleviated through natural treatments. This chapter explores various natural remedies and lifestyle practices to enhance skin health and address these conditions effectively.

1. Acne

Overview: Acne is a common skin condition characterized by pimples, blackheads, and whiteheads, primarily affecting the face, back, and shoulders. It can be caused by hormonal imbalances, poor diet, stress, and improper skincare.

Natural Treatments:

1. **Tea Tree Oil (Melaleuca alternifolia)**

   o **Active Compounds:** Terpinen-4-ol

   o **Uses:** Antibacterial and anti-inflammatory properties help reduce acne.

   o **Preparation and Application:** Dilute tea tree oil with a carrier oil (e.g., coconut oil) in a 1:10 ratio. Apply to the affected areas with a cotton swab twice daily.

   o **Precautions:** Always dilute before use. Conduct a patch test to check for allergic reactions.

2. **Aloe Vera (Aloe barbadensis)**

   o **Active Compounds:** Polysaccharides, gibberellins

   o **Uses:** Soothes inflammation, promotes healing, and reduces acne scars.

   o **Preparation and Application:** Apply fresh aloe vera gel directly from the plant to the affected areas. Leave it on for 20 minutes, then rinse with lukewarm water. Use twice daily.

   o **Precautions:** Generally safe for all skin types. Conduct a patch test if using for the first time.

3. **Honey and Cinnamon Mask**

   o **Active Compounds:** Honey (antibacterial), Cinnamon (anti-inflammatory)

   o **Uses:** Reduces bacteria and inflammation.

- o **Preparation and Application**: Mix 2 tablespoons of honey with 1 teaspoon of cinnamon to form a paste. Apply to the face, leave on for 10-15 minutes, then rinse off with warm water. Use 1-2 times a week.

- o **Precautions**: Conduct a patch test to check for allergic reactions.

2. Eczema

Overview: Eczema is a chronic skin condition characterized by itchy, inflamed, and dry skin. It can be triggered by allergens, stress, and environmental factors.

Natural Treatments:

1. **Oatmeal Baths**

   - o **Active Compounds**: Beta-glucans, saponins

   - o **Uses**: Soothes and moisturizes dry, itchy skin.

   - o **Preparation and Application**: Blend 1 cup of oatmeal into a fine powder and add it to a lukewarm bath. Soak for 15-20 minutes. Pat the skin dry gently. Use daily during flare-ups.

   - o **Precautions**: Ensure the bath water is lukewarm, not hot, to avoid further irritation.

2. **Coconut Oil (Cocos nucifera)**

   - o **Active Compounds**: Lauric acid, caprylic acid

   - o **Uses**: Moisturizes and reduces inflammation.

   - o **Preparation and Application**: Apply virgin coconut oil directly to the affected areas after bathing. Use 2-3 times daily.

   - o **Precautions**: Generally safe. Avoid if allergic to coconut.

3. **Chamomile Compress (Matricaria recutita)**

   - o **Active Compounds**: Bisabolol, flavonoids

   - o **Uses**: Reduces inflammation and soothes the skin.

   - o **Preparation and Application**: Brew a strong chamomile tea, soak a clean cloth in the tea, and apply it as a compress to the affected areas for 15-20 minutes. Use daily.

   - o **Precautions**: Conduct a patch test to check for allergic reactions.

3. Psoriasis

Overview: Psoriasis is an autoimmune condition that leads to the rapid buildup of skin cells, resulting in scaling and inflammation. It often appears on the elbows, knees, scalp, and lower back.

Natural Treatments:

1. **Turmeric (Curcuma longa)**

   o **Active Compounds:** Curcumin

   o **Uses:** Anti-inflammatory and antioxidant properties help reduce psoriasis symptoms.

   o **Preparation and Application:** Mix 1 teaspoon of turmeric powder with enough water to form a paste. Apply to the affected areas, leave on for 15 minutes, then rinse with warm water. Use daily.

   o **Precautions:** May stain the skin temporarily. Conduct a patch test before use.

2. **Aloe Vera (Aloe barbadensis)**

   o **Active Compounds:** Polysaccharides, gibberellins

   o **Uses:** Moisturizes, soothes, and reduces inflammation.

   o **Preparation and Application:** Apply fresh aloe vera gel directly to the affected areas. Leave it on for 30 minutes, then rinse with lukewarm water. Use 2-3 times daily.

   o **Precautions:** Generally safe for all skin types. Conduct a patch test if using for the first time.

3. **Apple Cider Vinegar (Acetic acid from apples)**

   o **Active Compounds:** Acetic acid

   o **Uses:** Helps restore the skin's pH balance and reduce itching.

   o **Preparation and Application:** Dilute apple cider vinegar with an equal amount of water. Apply to the affected areas with a cotton ball. Leave on for 10 minutes, then rinse with lukewarm water. Use daily.

   o **Precautions:** Avoid using on cracked or bleeding skin. Conduct a patch test before use.

4. Dry Skin

Overview: Dry skin can result from various factors, including environmental conditions, dehydration, and aging. It is characterized by rough, flaky, and itchy skin.

Natural Treatments:

1. **Honey (Apis mellifera)**

   o **Active Compounds**: Glucose, fructose, amino acids

   o **Uses**: Moisturizes and soothes dry skin.

   o **Preparation and Application**: Apply raw honey to the dry areas. Leave it on for 15-20 minutes, then rinse with warm water. Use 2-3 times a week.

   o **Precautions**: Generally safe. Avoid if allergic to honey.

2. **Olive Oil (Olea europaea)**

   o **Active Compounds**: Oleic acid, squalene

   o **Uses**: Moisturizes and nourishes the skin.

   o **Preparation and Application**: Apply extra virgin olive oil to the dry areas. Leave it on for 30 minutes, then rinse with lukewarm water. Use daily.

   o **Precautions**: Generally safe. Conduct a patch test to check for allergic reactions.

3. **Shea Butter (Vitellaria paradoxa)**

   o **Active Compounds**: Stearic acid, oleic acid

   o **Uses**: Deeply moisturizes and repairs the skin.

   o **Preparation and Application**: Apply shea butter to the dry areas after bathing. Use 2-3 times daily.

   o **Precautions**: Generally safe. Conduct a patch test to check for allergic reactions.

Holistic Practices for Skin Health

In addition to natural remedies, adopting holistic practices can significantly improve skin health. These practices align with nurturing the body and mind to achieve optimal wellness.

1. **Healthy Diet**

   o **Focus on Whole Foods**: Incorporate plenty of fruits, vegetables, whole grains, and lean proteins. Foods rich in antioxidants, such as berries, leafy greens, and nuts, can help protect the skin from damage.

   o **Hydrate**: Drink plenty of water to keep the skin hydrated and flush out toxins.

2. **Regular Exercise**

   o **Promote Blood Circulation**: Regular physical activity enhances blood flow, which helps nourish skin cells and keep them healthy.

   o **Reduce Stress**: Exercise helps reduce stress, which can improve skin conditions like acne and eczema.

3. **Adequate Sleep**

   o **Rest and Repair**: Aim for 7-8 hours of sleep per night to allow the skin time to repair and regenerate.

4. **Stress Management**

   o **Practice Relaxation Techniques**: Engage in activities like yoga, meditation, and deep breathing to manage stress and improve overall skin health.

5. **Proper Skincare Routine**

   o **Cleanse Gently**: Use a mild cleanser to remove dirt and impurities without stripping the skin of its natural oils.

   o **Moisturize Regularly**: Apply a suitable moisturizer to keep the skin hydrated and prevent dryness.

   o **Protect from Sun Damage**: Use sunscreen with at least SPF 30 to protect the skin from harmful UV rays.

Managing common skin conditions naturally involves a combination of herbal remedies, dietary changes, and holistic practices. By integrating these strategies into your daily routine, you can improve your skin health and overall well-being. Always consult with a healthcare professional before starting any new herbal regimen, especially if you have underlying health conditions or are on medication. Embrace these natural treatments and holistic practices, to achieve radiant and healthy skin.

Skincare Routines with Herbal Remedies

Skincare routines are an essential part of maintaining healthy, glowing skin. Incorporating herbal remedies into your daily regimen can enhance the benefits of your skincare routine, providing natural nourishment and healing properties. This section will guide you through creating effective skincare routines with herbal remedies for different skin types and concerns.

1. Morning Skincare Routine

Step 1: Cleansing

Herbal Remedy: Chamomile and Green Tea Cleanser

- **Ingredients**:
    - 1 cup of brewed chamomile tea
    - 1 cup of brewed green tea
    - 2 tablespoons of raw honey
    - 1 tablespoon of apple cider vinegar

Preparation and Use:

1. Brew chamomile and green tea and let them cool.
2. Mix the teas with honey and apple cider vinegar.
3. Store the mixture in a bottle and use it as a gentle cleanser in the morning.
4. Apply a small amount to your face, massage gently, and rinse with lukewarm water.

Benefits: Chamomile soothes and reduces inflammation, while green tea provides antioxidant protection. Honey moisturizes, and apple cider vinegar balances the skin's pH.

Step 2: Toning

Herbal Remedy: Rose and Witch Hazel Toner

- **Ingredients**:
    - 1 cup of rose water
    - 1/2 cup of witch hazel
    - 5 drops of lavender essential oil

Preparation and Use:

1. Mix rose water and witch hazel in a bottle.

2. Add lavender essential oil and shake well.

3. Apply the toner to your face with a cotton pad after cleansing.

Benefits: Rose water hydrates and soothes, witch hazel tightens pores and reduces inflammation, and lavender oil calms the skin.

Step 3: Moisturizing

Herbal Remedy: Aloe Vera and Jojoba Oil Moisturizer

- **Ingredients**:
    - 2 tablespoons of fresh aloe vera gel
    - 1 tablespoon of jojoba oil
    - 5 drops of tea tree oil (optional for acne-prone skin)

Preparation and Use:

1. Mix aloe vera gel and jojoba oil in a small bowl.

2. Add tea tree oil if desired and blend well.

3. Apply a small amount to your face and neck, gently massaging it into the skin.

Benefits: Aloe vera hydrates and heals, jojoba oil mimics the skin's natural oils, and tea tree oil helps prevent acne.

Step 4: Sun Protection

Herbal Remedy: Natural Sunscreen with Carrot Seed Oil

- **Ingredients**:
    - 1/4 cup of coconut oil
    - 1/4 cup of shea butter
    - 2 tablespoons of zinc oxide
    - 10 drops of carrot seed oil

Preparation and Use:

1. Melt coconut oil and shea butter in a double boiler.

2. Remove from heat and add zinc oxide and carrot seed oil.

3. Mix well and pour into a jar.

4. Apply a thin layer to your face and body before sun exposure.

Benefits: Carrot seed oil provides natural SPF, coconut oil and shea butter moisturize, and zinc oxide offers broad-spectrum sun protection.

2. Evening Skincare Routine

Step 1: Makeup Removal

Herbal Remedy: Calendula and Coconut Oil Makeup Remover

- **Ingredients**:
    o 1/4 cup of calendula-infused oil
    o 1/4 cup of coconut oil

Preparation and Use:

1. Combine calendula-infused oil and coconut oil in a bottle.

2. Shake well before use.

3. Apply a small amount to a cotton pad and gently wipe away makeup.

Benefits: Calendula heals and soothes the skin, while coconut oil effectively removes makeup and impurities.

Step 2: Cleansing

Use the same Chamomile and Green Tea Cleanser as in the morning routine.

Step 3: Exfoliation (2-3 times a week)

Herbal Remedy: Oatmeal and Honey Scrub

- **Ingredients**:
    o 2 tablespoons of finely ground oatmeal
    o 1 tablespoon of honey
    o 1 tablespoon of yogurt

Preparation and Use:

1. Mix oatmeal, honey, and yogurt to form a paste.

2. Apply to your face in circular motions, avoiding the eye area.

3. Rinse off with warm water.

Benefits: Oatmeal exfoliates gently, honey moisturizes, and yogurt contains lactic acid for additional exfoliation.

Step 4: Toning

Use the same Rose and Witch Hazel Toner as in the morning routine.

Step 5: Night Serum

Herbal Remedy: Rosehip and Frankincense Night Serum

- **Ingredients**:
    o 1 tablespoon of rosehip oil
    o 1 tablespoon of jojoba oil
    o 5 drops of frankincense essential oil

Preparation and Use:

1. Mix rosehip oil, jojoba oil, and frankincense oil in a dropper bottle.
2. Apply 3-4 drops to your face and neck, massaging gently.

Benefits: Rosehip oil promotes skin regeneration, jojoba oil nourishes, and frankincense oil reduces fine lines and improves skin tone.

Step 6: Moisturizing

Herbal Remedy: Shea Butter and Lavender Night Cream

- **Ingredients**:
    o 1/4 cup of shea butter
    o 1 tablespoon of almond oil
    o 5 drops of lavender essential oil

Preparation and Use:

1. Melt shea butter in a double boiler.
2. Remove from heat and stir in almond oil and lavender oil.
3. Pour into a jar and let it solidify.
4. Apply a small amount to your face and neck before bed.

Benefits: Shea butter deeply moisturizes and repairs the skin, almond oil nourishes, and lavender oil promotes relaxation and skin healing.

3. Weekly Skincare Treatments

Herbal Remedy: Detoxifying Clay Mask

- **Ingredients**:
    - 2 tablespoons of bentonite clay
    - 1 tablespoon of apple cider vinegar
    - 1 tablespoon of water
    - 5 drops of tea tree oil

Preparation and Use:

1. Mix bentonite clay with apple cider vinegar and water to form a paste.
2. Add tea tree oil and blend well.
3. Apply to your face, avoiding the eye area.
4. Leave on for 10-15 minutes, then rinse off with warm water.

Benefits: Bentonite clay detoxifies and cleanses the skin, while tea tree oil helps with acne and inflammation.

Herbal Remedy: Hydrating Herbal Facial Steam

- **Ingredients**:
    - 1 tablespoon of dried chamomile
    - 1 tablespoon of dried calendula
    - 1 tablespoon of dried lavender
    - 4 cups of boiling water

Preparation and Use:

1. Place dried herbs in a large bowl.
2. Pour boiling water over the herbs and let them steep for 5 minutes.
3. Drape a towel over your head and lean over the bowl to capture the steam.
4. Steam your face for 10-15 minutes.

Benefits: The steam opens pores, and the herbs hydrate and soothe the skin.

Integrating herbal remedies into your skincare routine can provide numerous benefits, promoting natural, healthy, and glowing skin. By following these detailed steps and incorporating the mentioned herbs, you can address various skin concerns while maintaining a holistic approach to skincare. Always remember to perform patch tests before using new ingredients and consult a healthcare professional if you have any skin conditions or allergies. These routines offer a natural and compassionate way to care for your skin.

Diet and Lifestyle for Radiant Skin

The journey to radiant skin begins from within. What we consume and how we live our daily lives significantly impact the health and appearance of our skin. By adopting a balanced diet rich in essential nutrients and integrating healthy lifestyle habits, we can support our skin's natural beauty and vitality. This section provides detailed guidance on the diet and lifestyle changes you can make to enhance your skin health.

1. Nutrient-Rich Diet for Radiant Skin

A. Antioxidant-Rich Foods Antioxidants protect the skin from damage caused by free radicals, which can lead to premature aging and dullness.

- **Berries**: Blueberries, strawberries, and raspberries are rich in vitamins C and E.

- **Leafy Greens**: Spinach, kale, and Swiss chard are packed with vitamins A, C, and K.

- **Nuts and Seeds**: Almonds, sunflower seeds, and flaxseeds provide vitamin E and omega-3 fatty acids.

B. Healthy Fats Healthy fats are crucial for maintaining skin elasticity and hydration.

- **Avocados**: High in monounsaturated fats and vitamins E and C.

- **Fatty Fish**: Salmon, mackerel, and sardines are excellent sources of omega-3 fatty acids.

- **Olive Oil**: Rich in antioxidants and healthy fats, ideal for drizzling over salads and vegetables.

C. Hydrating Foods Hydration is key to keeping skin plump and glowing.

- **Cucumbers**: High water content and silica for skin elasticity.

- **Watermelon**: Hydrating fruit with vitamins A and C.

- **Coconut Water**: Natural electrolytes for hydration and skin health.

D. Collagen-Boosting Foods Collagen is essential for skin firmness and elasticity.

- **Bone Broth**: Rich in collagen and amino acids.

- **Citrus Fruits**: Oranges, lemons, and grapefruits high in vitamin C to support collagen synthesis.

- **Bell Peppers**: Contain vitamin C and antioxidants to protect and boost collagen.

E. Detoxifying Foods Detoxifying foods help to cleanse the body and support liver function, which is essential for clear skin.

- **Beets**: High in antioxidants and nutrients that support liver detoxification.

- **Garlic**: Contains sulfur compounds that activate liver enzymes.

- **Green Tea**: Packed with antioxidants to help eliminate toxins.

2. Lifestyle Tips for Radiant Skin

A. Regular Exercise Exercise increases blood circulation, which helps to nourish skin cells and keep them healthy.

- **Cardio Workouts**: Running, cycling, and swimming to boost circulation and oxygenate the skin.

- **Strength Training**: Building muscle tone helps to maintain skin elasticity.

- **Yoga**: Promotes relaxation and reduces stress, which can improve skin conditions.

B. Stress Management Chronic stress can lead to skin issues such as acne, eczema, and psoriasis. Managing stress is crucial for maintaining healthy skin.

- **Mindfulness Meditation**: Practicing mindfulness can reduce stress hormones that negatively impact the skin.

- **Deep Breathing Exercises**: Techniques like diaphragmatic breathing can calm the nervous system.

- **Prayer and Spiritual Practices**: Incorporating prayer or spiritual practices can provide emotional comfort and reduce stress.

C. Adequate Sleep Sleep is the body's time to repair and regenerate. Poor sleep can lead to dull skin and dark circles.

- **Establish a Sleep Routine**: Going to bed and waking up at the same time every day helps regulate sleep cycles.

- **Create a Relaxing Bedtime Environment**: Ensure your bedroom is dark, cool, and quiet.

- **Avoid Screens Before Bed**: Limit exposure to blue light from phones and computers before sleep.

D. Hydration Drinking enough water is essential for keeping the skin hydrated and flushes out toxins.

- **Drink Plenty of Water**: Aim for at least 8 glasses of water per day.

- **Herbal Teas**: Chamomile, green tea, and dandelion tea can also help with hydration and provide additional skin benefits.

- **Limit Caffeine and Alcohol**: Both can dehydrate the skin, so moderation is key.

E. Skincare Routine Incorporate natural, herbal-based products in your skincare routine to support and maintain skin health.

- **Gentle Cleansing**: Use natural cleansers that do not strip the skin of its natural oils.

- **Exfoliation**: Regularly exfoliate with gentle, natural scrubs to remove dead skin cells.

- **Moisturization**: Use herbal-infused oils and creams to keep the skin hydrated and protected.

Achieving radiant skin is a holistic process that involves mindful eating, consistent lifestyle habits, and natural skincare practices. By following these detailed guidelines, you can nurture your skin from the inside out. Remember, the journey to healthy, glowing skin is a continuous process that requires dedication and care. Through balanced nutrition, regular exercise, effective stress management, proper hydration, and a thoughtful skincare routine, you can unlock the natural beauty of your skin and enjoy a vibrant, radiant complexion.

Chapter 10: Mental Health and Cognitive Function

Herbs for Mood and Mental Clarity

Mental health and cognitive function are crucial components of overall well-being. Herbs have been used for centuries to enhance mood and improve cognitive function, providing a natural and effective means to maintain mental health. In this chapter, we will explore various herbs that can help boost mood and sharpen mental clarity, along with their preparation methods, dosages, and safety considerations.

1. Ashwagandha (Withania somnifera)

Key Elements: Adaptogenic properties, stress relief, anxiety reduction

Active Compounds: Withanolides, alkaloids

Uses Against Diseases: Ashwagandha is known for its adaptogenic properties, which help the body manage stress. It can reduce symptoms of anxiety and depression, improve mood, and enhance cognitive function by reducing cortisol levels.

Preparation Methods, Dosage, Safety, and Precautions:

- **Preparation**: Ashwagandha can be taken as a powder, capsule, or tincture. It is commonly mixed with warm milk or water.

- **Dosage**: 300-500 mg of standardized extract, twice daily.

- **Safety and Precautions**: Generally safe for most people. However, it should be avoided during pregnancy and in individuals with hyperthyroidism.

2. Rhodiola (Rhodiola rosea)

Key Elements: Adaptogen, fatigue reduction, cognitive enhancer

Active Compounds: Rosavins, salidroside

Uses Against Diseases: Rhodiola helps the body adapt to stress, reduces fatigue, and enhances cognitive function. It is beneficial for improving mental performance, concentration, and reducing symptoms of depression.

Preparation Methods, Dosage, Safety, and Precautions:

- **Preparation**: Rhodiola is available in capsules, tablets, and tinctures. It can also be brewed as tea.

- **Dosage**: 200-400 mg of standardized extract daily.

- **Safety and Precautions**: Generally well-tolerated. It is recommended to take Rhodiola earlier in the day to avoid potential sleep disturbances.

3. Bacopa (Bacopa monnieri)

Key Elements: Memory enhancement, cognitive function, anxiety reduction

Active Compounds: Bacosides

Uses Against Diseases: Bacopa is traditionally used in Ayurvedic medicine to improve memory and cognitive function. It reduces anxiety and stress, enhances brain function, and promotes clarity and focus.

Preparation Methods, Dosage, Safety, and Precautions:

- **Preparation**: Bacopa can be consumed as a powder, capsule, or tincture. It is often taken with ghee or milk to enhance absorption.

- **Dosage**: 300-450 mg of standardized extract daily.

- **Safety and Precautions**: Generally safe but may cause digestive issues in some individuals. It should be used with caution in people with slow heart rates.

4. St. John's Wort (Hypericum perforatum)

Key Elements: Mood enhancement, depression relief, anxiety reduction

Active Compounds: Hypericin, hyperforin

Uses Against Diseases: St. John's Wort is widely used for its antidepressant properties. It is effective in treating mild to moderate depression and reducing symptoms of anxiety. It also helps to stabilize mood.

Preparation Methods, Dosage, Safety, and Precautions:

- **Preparation**: Available as capsules, tablets, teas, and tinctures.

- **Dosage**: 300 mg of standardized extract (0.3% hypericin) taken three times daily.

- **Safety and Precautions**: Can interact with various medications, including antidepressants, birth control pills, and blood thinners. Consult with a healthcare provider before use.

5. Ginkgo Biloba (Ginkgo biloba)

Key Elements: Cognitive enhancer, memory support, circulation improvement

Active Compounds: Flavonoids, terpenoids

Uses Against Diseases: Ginkgo Biloba enhances cognitive function by improving blood circulation to the brain. It supports memory, sharpens focus, and reduces symptoms of anxiety.

Preparation Methods, Dosage, Safety, and Precautions:

- **Preparation**: Ginkgo Biloba can be taken as capsules, tablets, teas, or tinctures.

- **Dosage**: 120-240 mg of standardized extract daily.

- **Safety and Precautions**: May cause headaches, dizziness, or gastrointestinal issues in some individuals. It can interact with blood-thinning medications, so consult with a healthcare provider before use.

6. Holy Basil (Ocimum sanctum)

Key Elements: Adaptogen, stress relief, cognitive enhancer

Active Compounds: Eugenol, rosmarinic acid, apigenin

Uses Against Diseases: Holy Basil, also known as Tulsi, helps reduce stress and anxiety, enhances cognitive function, and improves mental clarity. It is also known to support overall brain health.

Preparation Methods, Dosage, Safety, and Precautions:

- **Preparation**: Holy Basil can be consumed as a tea, capsule, or tincture.

- **Dosage**: 300-500 mg of standardized extract daily or 2-3 cups of tea.

- **Safety and Precautions**: Generally safe for most people. Pregnant women should consult with a healthcare provider before use.

7. Lemon Balm (Melissa officinalis)

Key Elements: Anxiety relief, cognitive enhancement, mood stabilizer

Active Compounds: Rosmarinic acid, flavonoids

Uses Against Diseases: Lemon Balm is effective in reducing anxiety, improving mood, and enhancing cognitive function. It can help with insomnia and promote relaxation.

Preparation Methods, Dosage, Safety, and Precautions:

- **Preparation**: Lemon Balm is available as tea, capsules, or tinctures.

- **Dosage**: 300-500 mg of standardized extract daily or 2-3 cups of tea.

- **Safety and Precautions**: Generally safe. May cause mild side effects such as nausea or headaches in some individuals.

8. Valerian (Valeriana officinalis)

Key Elements: Anxiety reduction, sleep aid, mood enhancement

Active Compounds: Valerenic acid, isovaleric acid

Uses Against Diseases: Valerian is commonly used to reduce anxiety, improve sleep quality, and enhance mood. It helps to relax the nervous system and alleviate symptoms of stress.

Preparation Methods, Dosage, Safety, and Precautions:

- **Preparation**: Available as capsules, tablets, teas, or tinctures.

- **Dosage**: 400-900 mg of standardized extract before bedtime.

- **Safety and Precautions**: Generally safe. May cause drowsiness, so it should not be taken before operating heavy machinery or driving.

9. Passionflower (Passiflora incarnata)

Key Elements: Anxiety relief, sleep aid, mood stabilizer

Active Compounds: Flavonoids, alkaloids

Uses Against Diseases: Passionflower is effective in reducing anxiety, improving sleep quality, and stabilizing mood. It helps to calm the mind and promote relaxation.

Preparation Methods, Dosage, Safety, and Precautions:

- **Preparation**: Passionflower can be consumed as tea, capsules, or tinctures.

- **Dosage**: 200-400 mg of standardized extract or 2-3 cups of tea daily.

- **Safety and Precautions**: Generally safe. May cause drowsiness, so it should not be taken before activities requiring alertness.

10. Lavender (Lavandula angustifolia)

Key Elements: Stress relief, anxiety reduction, cognitive enhancement

Active Compounds: Linalool, linalyl acetate

Uses Against Diseases: Lavender is widely known for its calming and relaxing properties. It helps reduce stress, alleviate anxiety, and improve cognitive function.

Preparation Methods, Dosage, Safety, and Precautions:

- **Preparation**: Lavender can be used as essential oil, tea, capsules, or tinctures.

- **Dosage**: 80-160 mg of standardized extract or 2-3 cups of tea daily.

- **Safety and Precautions**: Generally safe. Topical use of essential oil should be diluted to avoid skin irritation.

Incorporating these herbs into your daily routine can significantly enhance your mood and mental clarity. Always remember to consult with a healthcare provider before starting any new herbal regimen, especially if you are currently taking other medications or have pre-existing health conditions. By leveraging the natural power of these herbs, you can support your mental health and cognitive function effectively and safely.

Natural Approaches to Overcoming Insomnia

Insomnia, characterized by difficulty falling or staying asleep, affects millions and has far-reaching impacts on health and well-being. This chapter delves into natural remedies and lifestyle adjustments to combat insomnia effectively.

Understanding Sleep Mechanisms

Sleep is regulated by the circadian rhythm and the pineal gland's melatonin production, influenced by light exposure. Disruptions can lead to insomnia.

Diet and Nutrition

Proper nutrition is foundational for sleep health. Key dietary recommendations include:

- **Magnesium and Calcium**: These minerals support muscle relaxation and nervous system function. Foods rich in magnesium include leafy greens, nuts, seeds, and whole grains. Calcium can be found in dairy products, fortified plant-based milks, and leafy greens.

- **Avoid Stimulants**: Reduce or eliminate caffeine, sugar, and alcohol, especially in the evening, as they can interfere with sleep onset and quality.
- **Sleep-Promoting Foods**: Incorporate foods that promote sleep, such as almonds, bananas, and leafy greens. These foods contain tryptophan, magnesium, and potassium, which aid in relaxation and sleep induction.

Herbal Remedies

Herbal remedies offer a natural alternative to pharmaceutical sleep aids, with fewer side effects. Effective options include:

- **Valerian Root Tea**:
    - **Ingredients**: 1 teaspoon dried valerian root, 1 cup boiling water, honey (optional)
    - **Instructions**: Steep valerian root in boiling water for 10-15 minutes. Strain and add honey if desired. Drink 30-60 minutes before bedtime.

- **Chamomile Tea**:
    - **Ingredients**: 1 tablespoon dried chamomile flowers, 1 cup boiling water, honey or lemon (optional)
    - **Instructions**: Steep chamomile flowers in boiling water for 5-10 minutes. Strain and add honey or lemon to taste. Drink 30 minutes before bedtime.

- **Passionflower Tea**:
    - **Ingredients**: 1 teaspoon dried passionflower, 1 cup boiling water, honey (optional)
    - **Instructions**: Steep passionflower in boiling water for 10 minutes. Strain and sweeten with honey if desired. Drink 30 minutes before bedtime.

- **Lavender Tea**:
    - **Ingredients**: 1 teaspoon dried lavender buds, 1 cup boiling water, honey (optional)
    - **Instructions**: Steep lavender buds in boiling water for 5-10 minutes. Strain and add honey if desired. Drink in the evening.

Lifestyle Adjustments

Adopting certain lifestyle habits can significantly enhance sleep quality:

- **Consistent Sleep Schedule**: Going to bed and waking up at the same time every day helps regulate the body's internal clock.

- **Regular Exercise**: Physical activity promotes better sleep, but avoid vigorous exercise close to bedtime as it can be stimulating.

- **Evening Relaxation**: Establish a calming pre-sleep routine, such as gentle stretching, yoga, or reading a book.

Stress Management

Stress and anxiety are common contributors to insomnia. Effective stress management techniques include:

- **Meditation and Mindfulness**: These practices help calm the mind and reduce stress, making it easier to fall asleep.

- **Deep Breathing Exercises**: Deep breathing techniques can activate the parasympathetic nervous system, promoting relaxation.

- **Progressive Muscle Relaxation**: This technique involves tensing and then slowly relaxing each muscle group, helping to release physical tension.

Creating a Sleep-Conducive Environment

Optimizing your sleep environment is crucial for quality rest:

- **Dark, Cool, and Quiet**: Ensure your bedroom is dark, cool, and quiet. Use blackout curtains, earplugs, or a white noise machine if necessary.

- **Comfortable Bedding**: Invest in a comfortable mattress and pillows to support restful sleep.

- **Limit Blue Light Exposure**: Reduce exposure to blue light from electronic devices at least an hour before bedtime. Blue light can suppress melatonin production, making it harder to fall asleep.

Avoiding Sleep Medications

While sleep medications can provide short-term relief, they often come with side effects and the risk of dependency. Achieving restful sleep is possible through a combination of dietary changes, herbal remedies, lifestyle adjustments, and stress management techniques. By adopting these natural approaches, you can improve your sleep quality and overall well-being, paving the way for a healthier, more balanced life.

Reducing Anxiety and Stress Naturally

Anxiety and stress are prevalent in today's fast-paced world. This chapter delves into specific, practical steps you can take to alleviate anxiety and stress naturally.

Nutritional Support

Barbara O'Neill emphasizes the importance of nutrition in managing stress and anxiety.

- **Magnesium-Rich Foods**: Magnesium has a calming effect on the nervous system.
    - **Foods to Include**: Spinach, almonds, cashews, pumpkin seeds, and black beans.
    - **Instructions**: Incorporate a handful of nuts or a serving of leafy greens into your daily meals.

- **Omega-3 Fatty Acids**: These essential fats found in fish, flaxseeds, and walnuts help reduce inflammation and improve brain function.
    - **Foods to Include**: Salmon, chia seeds, and walnuts.
    - **Instructions**: Eat fatty fish like salmon twice a week or add a tablespoon of ground flaxseeds to your smoothies.

- **Hydration**: Dehydration can increase stress levels.
    - **Instructions**: Drink at least 8 cups of water daily. Carry a water bottle and set reminders to drink regularly.

Herbal Remedies

Using herbs can provide natural relief from anxiety and stress.

- **Passionflower**:
    - **Instructions**: Steep 1 teaspoon of dried passionflower in 1 cup of boiling water for 10 minutes. Strain and drink before bedtime.

- **Ashwagandha**:
    - **Instructions**: Take 500 mg of ashwagandha supplement daily or add 1 teaspoon of ashwagandha powder to a smoothie.

- **Lemon Balm**:
    - **Instructions**: Steep 1-2 teaspoons of dried lemon balm leaves in boiling water for 5-10 minutes. Strain and enjoy as a tea.

Aromatherapy

Aromatherapy uses essential oils to promote relaxation and reduce stress.

- **Lavender Oil:**

  o **Instructions:** Add a few drops of lavender oil to a diffuser or mix with a carrier oil and apply to your temples and wrists.

- **Bergamot Oil:**

  o **Instructions:** Add 3-4 drops to a warm bath or diffuse in your living space.

- **Chamomile Oil:**

  o **Instructions:** Use in a diffuser or add a few drops to a bath for a calming effect.

Physical Activity

Exercise is a powerful stress reliever and mood booster.

- **Yoga:**

  o **Instructions:** Practice yoga for at least 30 minutes, three times a week. Follow online classes or join a local studio.

- **Tai Chi:**

  o **Instructions:** Engage in tai chi sessions for 20-30 minutes daily to promote relaxation and balance.

- **Nature Walks:**

  o **Instructions:** Spend at least 20 minutes a day walking in nature to reduce stress levels.

Mindfulness and Meditation

Mindfulness and meditation practices help center the mind and reduce anxiety.

- **Mindfulness Meditation:**

  o **Instructions:** Spend 10-15 minutes each morning focusing on your breath. Sit quietly, close your eyes, and bring your attention to your breathing. When your mind wanders, gently bring it back to your breath.

- **Guided Imagery:**

- o **Instructions**: Use guided imagery recordings or apps to visualize calming and peaceful settings, helping to alleviate anxiety.

- **Gratitude Practice**:

  - o **Instructions**: Keep a gratitude journal and write down three things you are thankful for each day.

Stress Management Techniques

Incorporate these techniques into your daily routine to manage stress effectively.

- **Deep Breathing Exercises**:

  - o **Instructions**: Practice the 4-7-8 breathing technique. Inhale for 4 seconds, hold for 7 seconds, and exhale for 8 seconds. Repeat for 4-5 cycles.

- **Progressive Muscle Relaxation**:

  - o **Instructions**: Starting from your toes, tense each muscle group for 5 seconds, then slowly release. Move upward to your calves, thighs, abdomen, and so on.

- **Journaling**:

  - o **Instructions**: Write down your thoughts and feelings for 10 minutes each day to process emotions and reduce stress.

Creating a Relaxing Environment

Your surroundings can significantly impact your stress levels.

- **Declutter**:

  - o **Instructions**: Spend 15 minutes a day organizing and decluttering your space to promote a sense of calm.

- **Natural Light**:

  - o **Instructions**: Ensure your living space has plenty of natural light. Open curtains and blinds during the day.

- **Comfort Items**:

  - o **Instructions**: Incorporate items that bring you comfort, such as soft blankets, scented candles, or plants, to create a soothing environment.

Spiritual Practices and Prayer

Spirituality and prayer can provide comfort, purpose, and a sense of connection.

- **Daily Prayer**:

  - **Instructions**: Set aside time each day for prayer or spiritual reflection. Find a quiet place, close your eyes, and speak from your heart.

- **Spiritual Community**:

  - **Instructions**: Participate in a spiritual or religious community to build supportive relationships and find encouragement. Engage in group activities like study groups or service projects.

- **Meditative Prayer**:

  - **Instructions**: Combine meditation with prayer by focusing on a sacred word or phrase. Sit quietly and repeat the word or phrase, allowing it to bring you peace.

Reducing anxiety and stress naturally involves a holistic approach, integrating nutrition, herbal remedies, aromatherapy, physical activity, mindfulness, stress management techniques, a relaxing environment, and spiritual practices. By incorporating these strategies into your daily routine, you can enhance your mental health and overall well-being, leading to a more balanced and fulfilling life.

Chapter 11: Natural Solutions for Diverse Respiratory Conditions

Understanding Respiratory Health and Common Conditions

Respiratory health is fundamental to overall well-being. Our respiratory system is responsible for supplying oxygen to our body and removing carbon dioxide. Common respiratory conditions include asthma, bronchitis, sinusitis, and chronic obstructive pulmonary disease (COPD). This chapter is focused on the importance of natural remedies to support respiratory health, using herbs and holistic practices to alleviate symptoms and improve lung function.

Asthma

Understanding Asthma: Asthma is a chronic inflammatory condition of the airways that causes breathing difficulties. Symptoms include wheezing, shortness of breath, chest tightness, and coughing.

Herbal Remedies for Asthma

1. Licorice Root (Glycyrrhiza glabra)

- **Active Compounds**: Glycyrrhizin, flavonoids

- **Benefits**: Acts as an anti-inflammatory agent and helps soothe the airways.

- **Preparation and Use**:

  o **Tea**: Add 1 teaspoon of dried licorice root to a cup of boiling water. Steep for 10 minutes. Drink up to three times daily.

  o **Precautions**: Not recommended for prolonged use or in high doses due to potential side effects like high blood pressure. Avoid if pregnant or having heart conditions.

2. Mullein (Verbascum thapsus)

- **Active Compounds**: Saponins, mucilage

- **Benefits**: Helps clear mucus from the lungs and soothes the respiratory tract.

- **Preparation and Use**:

  o **Tea**: Steep 1-2 teaspoons of dried mullein leaves in a cup of boiling water for 10-15 minutes. Drink twice daily.

  o **Precautions**: Generally safe but ensure leaves are well strained to avoid throat irritation.

Bronchitis

Understanding Bronchitis: Bronchitis is the inflammation of the bronchial tubes, often resulting from a viral infection. Symptoms include a persistent cough, mucus production, fatigue, and shortness of breath.

Herbal Remedies for Bronchitis

1. Thyme (Thymus vulgaris)

- **Active Compounds**: Thymol, carvacrol

- **Benefits**: Antimicrobial and expectorant properties help clear mucus and fight infection.

- **Preparation and Use**:

    o **Tea**: Steep 1 teaspoon of dried thyme in a cup of boiling water for 10 minutes. Drink up to three times daily.

    o **Steam Inhalation**: Add a few drops of thyme essential oil to hot water and inhale the steam for 10 minutes.

    o **Precautions**: Generally safe for short-term use. Avoid during pregnancy.

2. Eucalyptus (Eucalyptus globulus)

- **Active Compounds**: Eucalyptol, cineole

- **Benefits**: Helps to clear congestion and acts as an anti-inflammatory.

- **Preparation and Use**:

    o **Steam Inhalation**: Add a few drops of eucalyptus oil to a bowl of hot water. Inhale the steam for 10 minutes.

    o **Chest Rub**: Mix eucalyptus oil with a carrier oil (like coconut oil) and apply to the chest for relief.

    o **Precautions**: Avoid using the essential oil directly on the skin without dilution.

Sinusitis

Understanding Sinusitis: Sinusitis is the inflammation of the sinus cavities, often caused by infections, allergies, or structural issues. Symptoms include nasal congestion, facial pain, headache, and a thick nasal discharge.

Herbal Remedies for Sinusitis

1. Peppermint (Mentha piperita)

- **Active Compounds**: Menthol, menthone

- **Benefits**: Acts as a decongestant and provides relief from sinus pressure.

- **Preparation and Use**:

  - **Steam Inhalation**: Add a few drops of peppermint oil to hot water and inhale the steam for 10 minutes.

  - **Tea**: Steep 1 teaspoon of dried peppermint leaves in a cup of boiling water for 10 minutes. Drink up to three times daily.

  - **Precautions**: Generally safe. May cause allergic reactions in sensitive individuals.

2. Goldenseal (Hydrastis canadensis)

- **Active Compounds**: Berberine, hydrastine

- **Benefits**: Antimicrobial properties help fight sinus infections and reduce inflammation.

- **Preparation and Use**:

  - **Tea**: Add 1 teaspoon of dried goldenseal root to a cup of boiling water. Steep for 10 minutes. Drink twice daily.

  - **Nasal Rinse**: Use a saline solution with a few drops of goldenseal tincture for nasal irrigation.

  - **Precautions**: Not recommended for prolonged use or during pregnancy.

Chronic Obstructive Pulmonary Disease (COPD)

Understanding COPD: COPD is a group of lung conditions, including emphysema and chronic bronchitis, that cause breathing difficulties. Symptoms include chronic cough, shortness of breath, frequent respiratory infections, and fatigue.

Herbal Remedies for COPD

1. Ginseng (Panax ginseng)

- **Active Compounds**: Ginsenosides, polysaccharides

- **Benefits**: Improves lung function and boosts energy levels.

- **Preparation and Use**:

  o **Tea**: Steep 1 teaspoon of dried ginseng root in a cup of boiling water for 15 minutes. Drink once daily.

  o **Capsules**: Available as supplements. Follow the dosage instructions on the product label.

  o **Precautions**: Consult with a healthcare provider before use, especially if on medications for diabetes or blood pressure.

2. Ginger (Zingiber officinale)

- **Active Compounds**: Gingerol, shogaol

- **Benefits**: Reduces inflammation and helps clear mucus from the lungs.

- **Preparation and Use**:

  o **Tea**: Steep 1 teaspoon of grated fresh ginger in a cup of boiling water for 10 minutes. Drink up to three times daily.

  o **Syrup**: Combine 1 tablespoon of fresh ginger juice with honey. Take 1 teaspoon twice daily.

  o **Precautions**: Generally safe. May cause heartburn or gastrointestinal discomfort in some individuals.

Practical Tips for Respiratory Health

1. Maintain a Healthy Diet: Include plenty of fruits, vegetables, whole grains, and lean proteins. Foods rich in antioxidants, like berries and leafy greens, help reduce inflammation and boost immune function.

2. Stay Hydrated: Drink plenty of water to keep the respiratory tract moist and help thin mucus secretions.

3. Avoid Irritants: Reduce exposure to pollutants, smoke, and allergens. Use air purifiers to maintain clean indoor air.

4. Practice Breathing Exercises: Techniques such as diaphragmatic breathing and pursed-lip breathing can improve lung function and oxygenation.

5. Stay Active: Regular physical activity strengthens respiratory muscles and enhances lung capacity.

6. Use a Humidifier: Adding moisture to the air can help ease breathing and reduce congestion, especially in dry environments.

Addressing respiratory conditions with natural remedies requires a holistic approach, combining herbal treatments with lifestyle changes. By incorporating these practical solutions into your daily routine, you can support your respiratory health and alleviate symptoms of common conditions. Always consult with a healthcare provider before starting any new treatment, especially if you have underlying health issues or are taking other medications. Through the power of nature, you can breathe easier and maintain optimal respiratory health.

Chapter 12: Natural Remedies for Allergies Healing

Understanding Respiratory Allergies

Respiratory allergies, such as allergic rhinitis and asthma, are conditions where the immune system overreacts to allergens like pollen, dust mites, pet dander, or mold. This overreaction causes symptoms such as sneezing, runny nose, itchy eyes, and difficulty breathing. Managing these allergies naturally involves addressing the root cause, supporting the immune system, and using natural remedies to alleviate symptoms.

The Holistic Approach to Allergy Management

A holistic approach to managing respiratory allergies, involves:

1. **Strengthening the Immune System**: A robust immune system can help reduce the severity of allergic reactions.

2. **Reducing Exposure to Allergens**: Minimizing contact with allergens can significantly reduce symptoms.

3. **Using Herbal Remedies**: Natural herbs can help alleviate symptoms and support overall respiratory health.

4. **Lifestyle Adjustments**: Diet, exercise, and stress management play crucial roles in managing allergies.

Strengthening the Immune System

A strong immune system is less likely to overreact to allergens. Here are some practical steps to bolster your immune health:

- **Diet**: Consume a diet rich in fruits, vegetables, nuts, seeds, and whole grains. These foods are packed with vitamins, minerals, and antioxidants that support immune function.

- **Hydration**: Drink plenty of water to keep the mucous membranes in your respiratory tract moist and healthy.

- **Sleep**: Ensure you get enough restorative sleep, as it is crucial for immune function.

- **Exercise**: Regular physical activity can help strengthen your immune system.

Reducing Exposure to Allergens

Minimizing exposure to allergens can help reduce the frequency and severity of allergic reactions. Consider the following tips:

- **Keep Windows Closed**: During high pollen seasons, keep windows closed to prevent pollen from entering your home.

- **Use Air Purifiers**: Air purifiers with HEPA filters can help reduce indoor allergens.

- **Regular Cleaning**: Regularly clean your home to remove dust, pet dander, and mold. Use a vacuum cleaner with a HEPA filter.

- **Wash Bedding Frequently**: Wash bedding in hot water to eliminate dust mites.

Herbal Remedies for Respiratory Allergies

Here are some effective herbal remedies to manage and heal respiratory allergies.

1. Nettle (Urtica dioica)

Active Compounds: Contains antihistamines and anti-inflammatory compounds.

Uses: Nettle can reduce the production of histamines, which cause allergy symptoms.

Preparation:

- **Nettle Tea**: Steep 1-2 teaspoons of dried nettle leaves in hot water for 10-15 minutes. Strain and drink up to three times a day.

- **Nettle Capsules**: Take according to the dosage instructions on the supplement packaging.

Precautions: Consult a healthcare provider if pregnant or nursing.

2. Butterbur (Petasites hybridus)

Active Compounds: Petasin and isopetasin, which reduce inflammation and block histamines.

Uses: Effective in treating hay fever and other allergic reactions.

Preparation:

- **Butterbur Capsules**: Take standardized extracts (free of pyrrolizidine alkaloids) as directed on the package.

Precautions: Ensure you use PA-free butterbur products to avoid liver toxicity.

3. Quercetin

Active Compounds: A flavonoid with antioxidant and antihistamine properties.

Uses: Reduces histamine release and inflammation.

Preparation:

- **Quercetin Supplements**: Take 500 mg up to twice daily, preferably with meals.
- **Quercetin-Rich Foods**: Incorporate foods like onions, apples, and berries into your diet.

Precautions: Consult a healthcare provider if pregnant or nursing.

4. Peppermint (Mentha piperita)

Active Compounds: Menthol, which acts as a natural decongestant and anti-inflammatory.

Uses: Helps clear nasal passages and reduce congestion.

Preparation:

- **Peppermint Tea**: Steep 1 teaspoon of dried peppermint leaves in hot water for 10 minutes. Strain and drink up to three times a day.
- **Peppermint Steam Inhalation**: Add a few drops of peppermint essential oil to a bowl of hot water, cover your head with a towel, and inhale the steam for 5-10 minutes.

Precautions: Not recommended for young children.

5. Eyebright (Euphrasia officinalis)

Active Compounds: Contains aucubin, an anti-inflammatory and antimicrobial compound.

Uses: Helps relieve itchy and watery eyes caused by allergies.

Preparation:

- **Eyebright Tea**: Steep 1 teaspoon of dried eyebright in hot water for 10 minutes. Strain and drink up to three times a day.
- **Eyebright Eye Wash**: Prepare a diluted tea solution, let it cool, and use it as an eye wash.

Precautions: Consult a healthcare provider before using as an eye wash.

Lifestyle Adjustments for Respiratory Health

In addition to herbal remedies, certain lifestyle changes can significantly improve respiratory health and reduce allergy symptoms.

1. Dietary Changes

- **Anti-Inflammatory Diet**: Include anti-inflammatory foods such as turmeric, ginger, garlic, and leafy greens in your diet.

- **Probiotics**: Consume probiotic-rich foods like yogurt, kefir, and sauerkraut to support gut health, which in turn can improve immune function.

- **Hydration**: Stay well-hydrated to keep mucous membranes moist and reduce irritation.

2. Regular Exercise

- **Outdoor Activities**: Engage in outdoor activities when pollen counts are low.

- **Breathing Exercises**: Practice deep breathing exercises to strengthen respiratory muscles and improve lung function.

3. Stress Management

- **Mindfulness and Meditation**: Practice mindfulness and meditation to reduce stress, which can exacerbate allergy symptoms.

- **Adequate Sleep**: Ensure you get enough sleep to support overall health and immune function.

Practical Tips for Daily Life

- **Nasal Rinse**: Use a saline nasal rinse daily to clear out allergens from your nasal passages.

- **Essential Oils**: Use essential oils like eucalyptus or lavender in a diffuser to reduce congestion and promote relaxation.

- **Humidifier**: Use a humidifier to maintain optimal humidity levels in your home, reducing dryness and irritation in the respiratory tract.

Managing respiratory allergies naturally involves a comprehensive approach that includes strengthening the immune system, reducing exposure to allergens, using herbal remedies, and making lifestyle adjustments. By incorporating these strategies into your daily routine, you can effectively manage and heal from respiratory allergies, improving your overall quality of life.

Chapter 13: Natural Solutions Against Chronic Inflammation

Understanding Chronic Inflammation

Chronic inflammation is a prolonged inflammatory response that can last for months or even years. It can lead to various health issues such as arthritis, cardiovascular diseases, diabetes, and autoimmune disorders.

Dietary Strategies for Reducing Inflammation

1. Anti-Inflammatory Foods

- **Fatty Fish**: Rich in omega-3 fatty acids, which reduce inflammation. Examples include salmon, mackerel, and sardines.

    o **Practical Tip**: Include fatty fish in your diet at least twice a week. Grill or bake to preserve the omega-3 content.

- **Leafy Greens**: Spinach, kale, and Swiss chard are packed with antioxidants and vitamins.

    o **Practical Tip**: Add a handful of leafy greens to your smoothies, salads, or soups daily.

- **Berries**: Blueberries, strawberries, and raspberries are high in antioxidants.

    o **Practical Tip**: Top your breakfast cereal or yogurt with fresh berries or enjoy them as a snack.

- **Nuts and Seeds**: Almonds, walnuts, flaxseeds, and chia seeds provide essential fatty acids and antioxidants.

    o **Practical Tip**: Sprinkle seeds on your salads, oatmeal, or smoothies. Snack on a handful of nuts.

- **Turmeric**: Contains curcumin, a powerful anti-inflammatory compound.

    o **Practical Tip**: Add turmeric to curries, soups, and teas. Combine with black pepper to enhance absorption.

2. Avoiding Inflammatory Foods

- **Refined Sugars and Carbohydrates**: These can trigger inflammatory responses.

    o **Practical Tip**: Reduce consumption of sugary drinks, pastries, and processed snacks. Opt for whole grains instead.

- **Trans Fats**: Found in many fried and processed foods.

  - **Practical Tip**: Avoid fast food and read labels to ensure products do not contain hydrogenated oils.

- **Excessive Alcohol**: Can contribute to inflammation and liver damage.

  - **Practical Tip**: Limit alcohol intake to moderate levels. Prefer red wine in small amounts, which contains resveratrol, an anti-inflammatory compound.

Herbal Remedies for Chronic Inflammation

1. Turmeric (Curcuma longa)

- **Active Compounds**: Curcumin

- **Benefits**: Reduces inflammation and oxidative stress.

- **Preparation and Use**:

  - **Golden Milk**: Mix 1 teaspoon of turmeric powder, a pinch of black pepper, and 1 cup of warm almond milk. Sweeten with honey if desired. Drink daily.

  - **Turmeric Paste**: Combine turmeric powder with coconut oil to form a paste. Apply to inflamed joints or muscles.

2. Ginger (Zingiber officinale)

- **Active Compounds**: Gingerol, shogaol

- **Benefits**: Anti-inflammatory and analgesic properties.

- **Preparation and Use**:

  - **Ginger Tea**: Grate 1-2 teaspoons of fresh ginger into a cup of boiling water. Steep for 10 minutes. Drink up to three times daily.

  - **Ginger Compress**: Mix grated ginger with hot water. Soak a cloth in the mixture and apply to the inflamed area.

3. Boswellia (Boswellia serrata)

- **Active Compounds**: Boswellic acids

- **Benefits**: Reduces inflammation and improves joint health.

- **Preparation and Use**:

  - **Boswellia Capsules**: Take 300-500 mg of Boswellia extract up to three times daily, following the product instructions.

- Boswellia Cream: Apply Boswellia cream to inflamed areas for topical relief.

4. Green Tea (Camellia sinensis)

- **Active Compounds**: Epigallocatechin gallate (EGCG)

- **Benefits**: Anti-inflammatory and antioxidant properties.

- **Preparation and Use**:

  - **Green Tea**: Brew 1 teaspoon of green tea leaves in a cup of hot water for 3-5 minutes. Drink 2-3 cups daily.

  - **Green Tea Compress**: Use cooled green tea bags as compresses on inflamed skin or joints.

5. Pineapple (Ananas comosus)

- **Active Compounds**: Bromelain

- **Benefits**: Reduces inflammation and aids in digestion.

- **Preparation and Use**:

  - **Fresh Pineapple**: Include fresh pineapple slices in your diet. Consume half a cup of pineapple daily.

  - **Bromelain Supplement**: Take bromelain supplements as directed, usually 200-400 mg three times daily.

Lifestyle Changes for Managing Inflammation

1. Regular Physical Activity

- **Benefits**: Exercise reduces inflammation and supports overall health.

- **Practical Tips**:

  - Engage in moderate exercise such as walking, swimming, or cycling for at least 30 minutes daily.

  - Include strength training exercises twice a week to maintain muscle mass and support joint health.

2. Stress Management

- **Benefits**: Reducing stress can lower inflammation levels in the body.

- **Practical Tips**:

- Practice mindfulness meditation, deep breathing exercises, or yoga regularly.
- Ensure you get adequate sleep, aiming for 7-8 hours per night.

3. Maintaining a Healthy Weight

- **Benefits**: Excess weight can increase inflammation and strain on joints.
- **Practical Tips**:
  - Follow a balanced diet rich in whole foods and low in processed items.
  - Monitor portion sizes and avoid overeating.

4. Hydration

- **Benefits**: Proper hydration helps to flush out toxins and reduce inflammation.
- **Practical Tips**:
  - Drink at least 8 cups (64 ounces) of water daily.
  - Include hydrating foods like cucumbers, oranges, and watermelons in your diet.

Practical Solutions and Instructions

1. Anti-Inflammatory Smoothie Recipe

- **Ingredients**:
  - 1 cup almond milk
  - 1 cup fresh pineapple chunks
  - 1 banana
  - 1 teaspoon turmeric powder
  - 1 teaspoon grated ginger
  - 1 handful of spinach
- **Instructions**:
  - Combine all ingredients in a blender.
  - Blend until smooth.
  - Enjoy once daily.

2. Turmeric-Ginger Anti-Inflammatory Tea

- **Ingredients**:
  - 1 teaspoon turmeric powder
  - 1 teaspoon grated ginger
  - 1 teaspoon honey
  - 2 cups water
- **Instructions**:
  - Bring water to a boil.
  - Add turmeric and ginger.
  - Simmer for 10 minutes.
  - Strain and add honey.
  - Drink twice daily.

3. Boswellia and Ginger Joint Rub

- **Ingredients**:
  - 2 tablespoons Boswellia powder
  - 1 tablespoon grated ginger
  - 2 tablespoons coconut oil
- **Instructions**:
  - Mix all ingredients to form a paste.
  - Apply to inflamed joints.
  - Leave on for 30 minutes, then rinse with warm water.
  - Use daily as needed.

Chapter 14: Natural Solutions for Cancer Prevention and Healing

Embracing Holistic Cancer Prevention and Healing

Cancer is one of the most daunting diagnoses one can face. Yet, many holistic practitioners, advocate for natural approaches to both prevent and aid in the healing process of cancer. This chapter explores detailed and practical solutions rooted in natural remedies, dietary adjustments, and lifestyle changes that support the body in its fight against cancer.

Understanding Cancer from a Holistic Perspective

Cancer develops when cells in the body begin to grow uncontrollably, forming tumors. These cells can invade other parts of the body, leading to severe health issues. An integrated approach combining nutrition, detoxification, immune support, and stress management can significantly contribute to cancer prevention and healing.

Nutritional Strategies for Cancer Prevention

1. Anti-Cancer Foods

- **Cruciferous Vegetables**: Broccoli, cauliflower, Brussels sprouts, and kale are rich in sulforaphane, which helps detoxify carcinogens.

    o **Practical Tip**: Include a serving of cruciferous vegetables in your meals daily. Steam or lightly sauté to preserve their nutrients.

- **Berries**: Blueberries, strawberries, and raspberries are high in antioxidants that protect cells from damage.

    o **Practical Tip**: Add fresh berries to your breakfast cereal, yogurt, or smoothies.

- **Garlic and Onions**: These contain sulfur compounds that boost the immune system's ability to fight cancer.

    o **Practical Tip**: Use fresh garlic and onions in cooking. Aim for at least one clove of garlic daily.

- **Green Tea**: Contains catechins, powerful antioxidants that have been shown to inhibit cancer growth.

    o **Practical Tip**: Drink 2-3 cups of green tea daily.

- **Turmeric**: Curcumin, the active ingredient in turmeric, has strong anti-inflammatory and anti-cancer properties.

o **Practical Tip**: Add turmeric to curries, soups, or make golden milk (see recipe below).

2. Alkaline Diet

Barbara O'Neill emphasizes the importance of maintaining an alkaline diet to create an inhospitable environment for cancer cells.

- **Practical Tip**: Focus on alkaline-forming foods such as leafy greens, fruits, nuts, seeds, and root vegetables. Minimize intake of acidic foods like meat, dairy, and processed foods.

3. Plant-Based Diet

A diet rich in plant-based foods can help reduce cancer risk.

- **Practical Tip**: Incorporate a variety of vegetables, fruits, whole grains, legumes, nuts, and seeds into your diet. Aim for at least five servings of vegetables and two servings of fruit daily.

Detoxification and Cancer Prevention

Detoxifying the body is crucial in preventing and combating cancer. Toxins can accumulate in the body and contribute to cancer development.

1. Liver Detox

The liver is the body's primary detox organ. Supporting liver function is essential for detoxification.

- **Practical Tip**: Use herbs like milk thistle, dandelion root, and turmeric to support liver health.
  - **Milk Thistle Tea**: Steep 1 teaspoon of milk thistle seeds in hot water for 10 minutes. Drink twice daily.
  - **Dandelion Root Tea**: Steep 1-2 teaspoons of dried dandelion root in hot water for 10 minutes. Drink twice daily.

2. Regular Detox Programs

Engage in regular detox programs to cleanse the body of toxins.

- **14-Day Detox Program** (see the dedicated chapter for the detailed program)
  - **Days 1-7**: Focus on raw fruits and vegetables, green juices, and herbal teas.
  - **Days 8-14**: Introduce light, steamed vegetables, whole grains, and legumes. Continue with herbal teas and green juices.

3. Avoiding Environmental Toxins

Reduce exposure to toxins in the environment.

- **Practical Tip**: Use natural cleaning products, avoid plastics, and use glass or stainless steel for food storage. Avoid pesticides by choosing organic produce when possible.

Herbal Remedies for Cancer Support

1. Essiac Tea

Essiac tea is a blend of herbs used traditionally to support cancer healing.

- **Ingredients**: Burdock root, sheep sorrel, slippery elm bark, and Indian rhubarb root.
- **Preparation**:
  - Combine equal parts of each herb.
  - Boil 1 tablespoon of the mixture in 1 quart of water for 10 minutes.
  - Let steep for 12 hours, then reheat and strain.
  - Drink 1-2 ounces daily on an empty stomach.

2. Turmeric and Black Pepper

Curcumin, the active compound in turmeric, has potent anti-cancer properties, and its absorption is enhanced by black pepper.

- **Ingredients**: 1 teaspoon turmeric powder, a pinch of black pepper.
- **Preparation**: Mix with a glass of warm water or add to food. Consume daily.

3. Green Tea Extract

Green tea extract contains concentrated amounts of catechins.

- **Dosage**: Follow the product instructions, typically 300-400 mg daily.
- **Practical Tip**: Choose a supplement with at least 50% EGCG (epigallocatechin gallate).

Lifestyle Changes for Cancer Prevention and Healing

1. Regular Exercise

Exercise boosts the immune system and helps maintain a healthy weight.

- **Practical Tip**: Aim for at least 30 minutes of moderate exercise, such as walking, swimming, or cycling, five times a week.

2. Stress Management

Chronic stress can weaken the immune system. Techniques like meditation, yoga, and deep breathing can help manage stress.

- **Practical Tip**: Practice mindfulness meditation for 10-15 minutes daily. Engage in activities that promote relaxation, such as gardening, reading, or listening to music.

3. Adequate Sleep

Quality sleep is essential for immune function and overall health.

- **Practical Tip**: Aim for 7-8 hours of sleep per night. Create a restful bedtime routine, avoid screens before bed, and keep your sleep environment cool and dark.

4. Avoiding Carcinogens

Minimize exposure to known carcinogens such as tobacco smoke, excessive alcohol, and processed meats.

- **Practical Tip**: Quit smoking and limit alcohol consumption. Choose fresh, whole foods over processed options.

Practical Solutions and Instructions

Golden Milk Recipe

- **Ingredients**:
    - 1 cup almond milk
    - 1 teaspoon turmeric powder
    - 1/4 teaspoon black pepper
    - 1/2 teaspoon cinnamon
    - 1 teaspoon honey (optional)
- **Instructions**:
    - Combine all ingredients in a saucepan.
    - Heat gently, stirring continuously, until warm.
    - Pour into a cup and enjoy daily.

Berry Antioxidant Smoothie

- **Ingredients**:
  - 1 cup mixed berries (blueberries, strawberries, raspberries)
  - 1 banana
  - 1 cup spinach
  - 1 tablespoon ground flaxseed
  - 1 cup almond milk
- **Instructions**:
  - Combine all ingredients in a blender.
  - Blend until smooth.
  - Drink once daily.

Green Detox Juice

- **Ingredients**:
  - 1 cucumber
  - 2 celery stalks
  - 1 handful of spinach
  - 1 apple
  - 1 lemon
  - 1-inch piece of ginger
- **Instructions**:
  - Juice all ingredients.
  - Stir well and drink immediately.
  - Consume once daily for detox support.

By integrating these dietary, herbal, and lifestyle strategies, you can support your body in preventing and healing from cancer. Holistic approach emphasizes the importance of nurturing the body, mind, and spirit to create an environment where healing can thrive. Always consult with a healthcare professional before starting any new treatment, especially if you are undergoing conventional cancer treatments.

Chapter 15: Specific Nutrients against common ailments

Understanding the specific nutrients that combat common ailments is key to empowering your self-healing journey. Barbara O'Neill often emphasizes the therapeutic power of nature's bounty in addressing health concerns. In this chapter, we will detail specific nutrients, their sources, and how they can help prevent or manage common ailments.

1. Vitamin C for Immune Support

Why it's important: Vitamin C is essential for the growth and repair of tissues, acts as an antioxidant, and boosts the immune system.

Sources:

- Citrus fruits (oranges, lemons, grapefruits)

- Berries (strawberries, blueberries, raspberries)

- Kiwi

- Bell peppers

- Broccoli

- Brussels sprouts

How to incorporate:

- Start your day with a glass of warm water with lemon.

- Add berries to your breakfast cereal or yogurt.

- Snack on bell pepper slices with hummus.

- Include broccoli and Brussels sprouts in your lunch or dinner meals.

2. Omega-3 Fatty Acids for Heart Health

Why it's important: Omega-3 fatty acids reduce inflammation, lower blood pressure, and decrease the risk of heart disease.

Sources:

- Fatty fish (salmon, mackerel, sardines)

- Flaxseeds and flaxseed oil

- Chia seeds

- Walnuts

- Algal oil (for a plant-based option)

How to incorporate:

- Have a serving of fatty fish at least twice a week.

- Add flaxseeds or chia seeds to smoothies, oatmeal, or salads.

- Snack on a handful of walnuts.

- Use algal oil supplements if you are vegetarian or vegan.

3. Magnesium for Muscle and Nerve Function

Why it's important: Magnesium supports muscle and nerve function, regulates blood sugar levels, and promotes a calm nervous system.

Sources:

- Leafy green vegetables (spinach, kale)

- Nuts and seeds (almonds, pumpkin seeds)

- Legumes (black beans, chickpeas)

- Whole grains (brown rice, quinoa)

- Dark chocolate

How to incorporate:

- Make a green smoothie with spinach or kale.

- Snack on almonds or pumpkin seeds.

- Include legumes in soups, stews, or salads.

- Opt for whole grains over refined grains.

- Enjoy a small piece of dark chocolate as a treat.

4. Zinc for Wound Healing and Immunity

Why it's important: Zinc is crucial for immune function, wound healing, and DNA synthesis.

Sources:

- Shellfish (oysters, crab)

- Meat (beef, chicken)

- Legumes (lentils, chickpeas)

- Seeds (hemp seeds, sesame seeds)

- Nuts (cashews, almonds)

How to incorporate:

- Include a serving of shellfish or meat in your meals a few times a week.

- Add legumes to soups, stews, or salads.

- Sprinkle seeds over yogurt, oatmeal, or salads.

- Snack on a handful of nuts.

5. Calcium for Bone Health

Why it's important: Calcium is vital for bone and teeth health, muscle function, and nerve signaling.

Sources:

- Dairy products (milk, cheese, yogurt)

- Leafy greens (collard greens, broccoli)

- Fortified plant-based milks (almond milk, soy milk)

- Sardines and canned salmon (with bones)

- Tofu

How to incorporate:

- Have a serving of dairy or fortified plant-based milk with breakfast.

- Include leafy greens in your meals as side dishes or in smoothies.

- Add canned salmon to salads or sandwiches.

- Use tofu in stir-fries or soups.

6. Iron for Energy and Hemoglobin Production

Why it's important: Iron is essential for hemoglobin production, which transports oxygen in the blood, and supports energy levels.

Sources:

- Red meat (beef, lamb)
- Poultry (chicken, turkey)
- Seafood (clams, shrimp)
- Legumes (lentils, beans)
- Spinach and other leafy greens

How to incorporate:

- Include a serving of meat or poultry in your meals a few times a week.
- Add seafood to pasta dishes, salads, or as a main course.
- Use legumes in soups, stews, or as side dishes.
- Make salads with spinach or add it to smoothies.

7. Vitamin D for Immune and Bone Health

Why it's important: Vitamin D supports immune function, bone health, and reduces inflammation.

Sources:

- Sunlight exposure
- Fatty fish (salmon, mackerel)
- Egg yolks
- Fortified foods (orange juice, cereals)
- Mushrooms exposed to sunlight

How to incorporate:

- Spend 10-30 minutes in the sun several times a week.

- Include fatty fish in your meals.

- Add egg yolks to your breakfast routine.

- Choose fortified foods as part of your diet.

- Use mushrooms in soups, salads, or as side dishes.

8. Folate for Cell Function and Tissue Growth

Why it's important: Folate is crucial for DNA synthesis, cell division, and tissue growth.

Sources:

- Leafy green vegetables (spinach, kale)

- Citrus fruits (oranges, lemons)

- Beans and legumes (black beans, lentils)

- Fortified cereals and grains

- Avocados

How to incorporate:

- Make salads with leafy greens.

- Snack on citrus fruits or add them to your meals.

- Use beans and legumes in various dishes like soups, stews, or salads.

- Choose fortified cereals for breakfast.

- Include avocados in salads, sandwiches, or as a topping.

9. Vitamin E for Skin and Eye Health

Why it's important: Vitamin E acts as an antioxidant, protecting cells from damage, and is important for skin and eye health.

Sources:

- Nuts and seeds (almonds, sunflower seeds)

- Spinach and broccoli

- Vegetable oils (sunflower oil, safflower oil)

- Fortified cereals

- Avocado

How to incorporate:

- Snack on nuts and seeds or add them to dishes.

- Include spinach and broccoli in your meals.

- Use vegetable oils in cooking and dressings.

- Choose fortified cereals for breakfast.

- Add avocado to salads, sandwiches, or smoothies.

10. Probiotics for Gut Health

Why it's important: Probiotics support a healthy gut microbiome, aiding digestion and boosting immunity.

Sources:

- Yogurt and kefir

- Sauerkraut and kimchi

- Miso and tempeh

- Kombucha

- Pickles

How to incorporate:

- Have yogurt or kefir as a snack or with breakfast.

- Include fermented vegetables like sauerkraut and kimchi in meals.

- Use miso and tempeh in soups, stews, or stir-fries.

- Drink kombucha as a refreshing beverage.

- Snack on pickles or add them to sandwiches.

By incorporating these specific nutrients into your diet, you can address and prevent common ailments naturally. Each nutrient plays a vital role in maintaining overall health, and through mindful dietary choices, you can support your body's self-healing capabilities effectively.

Chapter 16: 15 Transformative Juice Blends for Detox, Energy, and Immunity

Juicing is a fantastic way to combine various fruits and vegetables for detoxification, a boost in energy, and enhanced immunity. Here are five transformative juice blends, each designed to target specific wellness goals. Each recipe yields about one serving, ideal for immediate consumption to maximize nutrient intake.

1. Green Detox Delight

Ingredients:

- 2 cups spinach

- 1 green apple, cored and sliced

- 1/2 cucumber

- 1 celery stalk

- Juice of 1/2 lemon

- 1 inch piece of ginger, peeled

Instructions:

1. Wash all produce thoroughly.

2. Peel the lemon and ginger, and prepare the other ingredients for juicing.

3. Juice all ingredients, starting with the ginger and followed by the leafy greens, to maximize yield.

4. Stir the lemon juice into the blended juice for an extra detoxifying effect and enjoy immediately.

Benefits: This juice blend is packed with antioxidants, aids in digestion, and helps to cleanse the liver.

2. Tropical Energy Booster

Ingredients:

- 1 cup fresh pineapple chunks

- 1 orange, peeled

- 1/2 mango, peeled and pitted

- 1/2 banana

Instructions:

1. Prepare all fruits by cutting them into sizes that can fit through your juicer.

2. Juice the pineapple, orange, and mango.

3. Pour the juice into a blender, add the banana, and blend until smooth.

4. Enjoy this tropical drink to kickstart your morning with a burst of energy.

Benefits: High in Vitamin C and natural sugars, it boosts energy levels and provides a hydrating effect.

3. Beetroot Immunity Elixir

Ingredients:

- 1 medium beet, peeled and sliced

- 1 carrot, peeled and chopped

- 1 apple, cored and sliced

- Juice of 1/2 lemon

- 1 inch piece of turmeric, peeled

Instructions:

1. Prep all ingredients by peeling and appropriately sizing them for your juicer.

2. Juice the beet, carrot, apple, and turmeric sequentially.

3. Stir in the lemon juice to enhance flavor and nutrient absorption.

4. Drink immediately to support immune function and reduce inflammation.

Benefits: Rich in vitamins and minerals, this juice improves blood flow and boosts the immune system.

4. Antioxidant Berry Flush

Ingredients:

- 1 cup blueberries

- 1 cup strawberries, hulled

- 1/2 cup raspberries

- 1 cup water or coconut water

Instructions:

1. Wash all berries thoroughly.

2. Juice the berries. If your juicer handles soft fruits poorly, blend them instead and then strain the mixture.

3. Mix the berry juice with water or coconut water to make it more hydrating.

4. Consume this refreshing juice to aid in detoxification and promote skin health.

Benefits: Loaded with antioxidants, this juice helps in neutralizing free radicals and detoxifying the body.

5. Spicy Citrus Immune Boost

Ingredients:

- 2 oranges, peeled

- 1 grapefruit, peeled

- 1/2 lime, peeled

- 1/2 inch piece of ginger, peeled

- A pinch of cayenne pepper

Instructions:

1. Juice the oranges, grapefruit, lime, and ginger.

2. Sprinkle cayenne pepper into the juice and stir well.

3. Drink this potent blend to boost vitamin intake and enhance immune defense.

Benefits: The vitamin C from the citrus and the anti-inflammatory properties of ginger and cayenne pepper make this an excellent choice for boosting immunity and metabolism.

6. Cooling Cucumber Mint Cleanse

Ingredients:

- 1 large cucumber

- 1 green apple, cored and sliced

- 1/2 cup fresh mint leaves
- 1/2 lime, peeled
- 1 inch piece of ginger, peeled

Instructions:

1. Thoroughly wash cucumber, apple, mint, and lime.
2. Juice the cucumber, apple, ginger, and lime together.
3. Add the mint leaves last to ensure their fresh flavor is maximally extracted.
4. Serve chilled for a refreshing and cleansing beverage.

Benefits: This juice is hydrating, aids in digestion, and has a cooling effect, making it perfect for hot days or after workouts.

7. Sweet Potato Sunrise

Ingredients:

- 1 medium sweet potato, peeled and sliced
- 2 large carrots, peeled
- 1 orange, peeled
- 1/2 teaspoon cinnamon

Instructions:

1. Juice the sweet potato, carrots, and orange.
2. Stir in cinnamon for a comforting spice touch.
3. Enjoy this nutrient-dense juice in the morning for a gentle start with a sweet, earthy flavor.

Benefits: Rich in beta-carotene and vitamins, this juice supports eye health and immune function with a warming cinnamon twist.

8. Power Green Kick

Ingredients:

- 2 cups kale leaves
- 1/2 cup parsley

- 1 green apple, cored and sliced

- 1 cucumber

- 1/2 lemon, peeled

- 1 inch piece of ginger, peeled

Instructions:

1. Wash all greens thoroughly.

2. Juice kale, parsley, apple, cucumber, lemon, and ginger sequentially.

3. Stir well and drink immediately to harness the most from its nutrient-rich profile.

Benefits: This powerful green juice detoxifies, boosts energy, and enhances overall vitality with a high concentration of antioxidants and vitamins.

9. Red Radiance Booster

Ingredients:

- 1 medium beet, peeled and sliced

- 1 red apple, cored and sliced

- 1/2 cup red cabbage, chopped

- 1/2 lemon, peeled

- 1 carrot, peeled

Instructions:

1. Prep all ingredients by peeling and slicing them as needed.

2. Juice the beet, apple, cabbage, lemon, and carrot.

3. Mix well and enjoy this vibrant, colorful juice.

Benefits: Loaded with antioxidants and vitamin C, this juice aids in reducing inflammation, boosting heart health, and increasing energy levels.

10. Pineapple Ginger Hydrator

Ingredients:

- 1 cup pineapple chunks

- 1/2 cucumber

- 1 inch piece of ginger, peeled

- 1/2 lime, peeled

Instructions:

1. Prepare all ingredients and juice them together, starting with the ginger to get its full flavor.

2. Enjoy this tropical, zesty juice any time of day for a refreshing treat.

Benefits: Pineapple provides bromelain, an enzyme that aids digestion, while ginger offers anti-inflammatory benefits, making this juice perfect for post-exercise recovery or general hydration.

11. Citrus Carrot Glow

Ingredients:

- 3 large carrots, peeled

- 2 oranges, peeled

- 1 lemon, peeled

- 1 inch piece of turmeric, peeled

Instructions:

1. Wash and peel the carrots, oranges, lemon, and turmeric.

2. Juice the carrots, oranges, lemon, and turmeric.

3. Stir well and enjoy this bright and revitalizing juice.

Benefits: This juice is packed with vitamin A and C, antioxidants, and anti-inflammatory properties from turmeric, promoting a healthy glow and boosting the immune system.

12. Spiced Apple Delight

Ingredients:

- 2 red apples, cored and sliced

- 1 inch piece of ginger, peeled

- 1/2 teaspoon cinnamon

- 1/4 teaspoon nutmeg

- 1/4 cup water

Instructions:

1. Juice the apples and ginger together.

2. Add the juice to a blender with water, cinnamon, and nutmeg. Blend until smooth.

3. Serve chilled or over ice for a spiced and refreshing drink.

Benefits: Apples and ginger aid digestion and reduce inflammation, while the spices add warmth and boost metabolism.

13. Berry Beet Blast

Ingredients:

- 1 medium beet, peeled and sliced

- 1 cup strawberries

- 1/2 cup blueberries

- 1/2 cup raspberries

- Juice of 1/2 lemon

Instructions:

1. Prepare and wash all the berries and beet.

2. Juice the beet and berries together.

3. Stir in the lemon juice and serve immediately.

Benefits: This juice is a powerhouse of antioxidants, vitamins, and minerals, supporting detoxification, reducing inflammation, and enhancing cardiovascular health.

14. Tropical Greens Fusion

Ingredients:

- 1 cup fresh pineapple chunks

- 1/2 cup kale leaves

- 1/2 cup spinach leaves

- 1/2 cucumber

- 1/2 lime, peeled

Instructions:

1. Wash and prepare all the ingredients.

2. Juice the pineapple, kale, spinach, cucumber, and lime.

3. Mix well and enjoy this tropical and nutritious blend.

Benefits: This juice combines the sweetness of pineapple with the nutrient-rich greens, providing a refreshing detox with a boost of vitamins and minerals.

15. Cucumber Melon Refresher

Ingredients:

- 1 cup honeydew melon chunks

- 1/2 cucumber

- 1/2 green apple, cored and sliced

- Juice of 1/2 lime

- Fresh mint leaves (optional)

Instructions:

1. Prepare and wash the melon, cucumber, and apple.

2. Juice the honeydew melon, cucumber, and apple together.

3. Stir in the lime juice and garnish with fresh mint leaves if desired.

Benefits: This hydrating juice is perfect for hot days, providing a refreshing and light drink rich in vitamins and antioxidants that help detoxify and hydrate the body.

GET YOUR EXCLUSIVE BONUS HERE!

SCAN THIS QR CODE:

OR

COPY AND PASTE THIS URL:

https://drive.google.com/drive/folders/1E6Y0HPW0c X4MCR2f9WZkNYx7m2jTBJCx?usp=sharing

Made in United States
North Haven, CT
05 September 2024